STATISTICAL SPORTS MODELS IN EXCEL

VOLUME II

ANDREW MACK

❀ Created with Vellum

CONTENTS

BAYES & ANECDOTAL THOUGHTS

INTRODUCTION

"Would you like me to give you a formula for success? It's quite simple, really. Double your rate of failure. You're thinking of failure as the enemy of success. But it isn't at all, you can be discouraged by failure – or you can learn from it. So go ahead and make mistakes. Make all you can. Because remember that's where you'll find success. On the far side of failure."

— THOMAS J. WATSON

Sports modelling is one of the ultimate intellectual challenges. It involves the application of careful, reasoned skill in the face of considerable parameter uncertainty. As you've likely discovered, there is a lot more to it than simply picking a winning team.

While the process of wagering itself is associated with the psychological pressures of risk and loss aversion, building sports models presents a new challenge: testing your ability to persevere in the face of repeated failures.

There is an expression that says an expert is someone that has made every mistake that can be made in a very narrow field. While I would naturally hesitate to call myself an expert, I have personally learned a great deal from my own mistakes in the narrow field of sports modelling. Perhaps surprisingly, I have enjoyed almost every moment of it - because when an idea hasn't worked out I've been able to leverage that experience to imagine better possible solutions in the future.

If you take a similarly inquisitive approach and view modelling failures not as setbacks but as Henry Ford once said, *"an opportunity to begin again more intelligently"*, I am confident you will eventually arrive at your own viable solutions to the various modelling challenges in the arena of your choice. In that sense, modelling setbacks are never really failures in the final analysis provided you continue to refine your process and refuse to give up.

With that, I would like to officially welcome you to *Statistical Sports Models in Excel Volume 2.*

Following up where the first book left off, this second volume aims to provide you with more tools, techniques and ideas that can be used to take your sports modelling efforts to the next level using beginner-friendly Excel. Of particular interest this time around will be moving past generalized team models and into player based concepts, derivatives and prop bets. Some of the ideas presented are slightly more experimental than before, but I think you'll find them equally useful.

Because some of the areas of discussion concern markets I am currently betting with my own models, I have had to walk a very fine line between providing genuinely useful information and preserving my current sources of expected value. It's been a visceral reminder that nobody can deliver a market-ready model to you wrapped in a red ribbon. To do so would immediately raise the bar for a given market, rendering the formerly useful model now lagging behind the current field of competition.

That's a lose-lose scenario for everyone, so understandably I would be ill-advised to do that. What I *can do* however is show you my past work - the models I've built along the way. In this sense you can benefit from my impressive litany of setbacks and errors, which in time can speed up your learning curve provided you are willing to take the tools provided and continue the search for market value on your own.

It's safe to assume that if a model is contained in this book, I have devised something in R/Python that is more effective than what I've shared here. This doesn't mean there is no value in the models - far from it. It simply means that there will be some room (and necessity) for you to take these models and make them your own with various modifications. What I've presented isn't the only solution to each given scenario, and in some cases it might not necessarily be the best. It is however *one possible solution* - providing you with a template to begin your own investigation. You may well end up producing something even better. I will be the first to congratulate you when you do.

The ultimate goal in walking readers through downloadable spreadsheet models is to provide you with a thought process, a development process that you can take and apply in your own way to your preferred market. In doing so, when you create a successful model, it will be uniquely yours - which preserves its value to you.

The same caveats from *Statistical Sports Models in Excel Volume 1* still apply - I'm not classically trained in any of the methodologies I'm presenting, and errors or accidental omissions are a possibility. Should you find one, please be in contact with me on Twitter - I would as always welcome your constructive feedback.

Finally, you should also know that some of my ideas in the later sections of the book are anecdotal, speculative or of the N=1 variety. I have included them because I believe they will be of use to you, which was a general sentiment I received when reaching out to readers of SSME1 for their feedback. As with all of the material here, try ideas out for yourself. Weigh the evidence. Conduct your own tests. See if you can spot weaknesses and come up with something better.

With all that being said, I think it's time to get into a spreadsheet. Let's fire up Excel and get back to work.

As Jon Gruden likes to say, *"knock on wood if you're with me."*

Andrew Mack | @Gingfacekillah

GROUNDWORK

1

ASSESSING MARKET STRENGTH

In my first book as well as in subsequent podcasts, I've frequently suggested that novice sports modellers focus on markets with low limits that are significantly easier to beat. Starting in these areas can provide an essential morale boost as you build the skills and experience to model more highly liquid markets.

Despite this, I regularly receive questions on Twitter about popular but difficult markets and crafting modelling approaches for them: the NFL, NBA, MLB and others. Readers overwhelmingly want to take a shot at their favourite major sport, competition level be damned.

I can certainly respect their enthusiasm, so let's give it a shot together.

If we are going to have any hope of success we might first consider exactly what we're dealing with. We should start by sizing up the competition and testing it for Root Mean Squared Error [RMSE], Mean Absolute Error [MAE] and Log Loss against the actual game results. This should give us a decent sense of the aggregate market's efficiency and what metric benchmarks we might have to beat in order to have a reasonable expectation of profit.[1]

The first thing we should always want to know is how strong [or accurate] our relative competition is. Once we know that, we have something to compare a future model to - so it's a logical place to start when assessing your prospects in any sport. Let's do that now with the NBA to see just how challenging a major market is to beat.

STEP 1: GATHER SOME ODDS DATA

The first thing we'll need is historical odds data. The preferred method for obtaining odds data is generally by employing some form of web scraping using either R or Python. This is outside the scope of this book however, so let's gather some data from a more easily accessible source:

https://www.sportsbookreviewsonline.com

Clicking on "Scores & Odds Archives" on the left sidebar will take you to a page where you can select a sport and download historical odds data by year. [2] One problem though with free sources like this is that it isn't always disclosed which sportsbook(s) the historical odds are coming from, which means that if we beat the benchmarks we establish it would still be unclear precisely *where* we should place a wager. It's also fairly common for free sources to contain strange formatting or errors that necessitate more data wrangling work. On the plus side though, it's free.

One question we face is how much data to collect. Generally more data is better for statistical analysis, but for this test I'm only going to take the last 2 years of odds data. I personally think that blending market efficiency from the last 10 years together might not be the best approach, since we're interested in how accurate or efficient the market has been recently. Additionally, changes to game rules can also impact the efficiency of the market and it might not be the best idea to blend multiple eras of the game together. For whatever sport you're testing, you may want to consider these factors when deciding how much data to use in your experiments.

STEP 2: FORMAT & CLEAN THE DATA

Once we've downloaded the data we're interested in we need to clean and format it. For the most part, this means removing rows with blank cells and organizing the columns so that we can test for our benchmarks. You'll see that I've already completed this in the accompanying "Assessing Market Strength" spreadsheet file. The data columns I have used in the sheet are:

- Away Points
- Home Points
- Total Points Closing Line
- Actual Total
- Home Actual Margin of Victory [MOV]
- Home Win [binary value where 1 indicates a home win]
- Away Moneyline US Odds
- Away Closing Pointspread
- Home Moneyline US Odds
- Home Closing Pointspread
- Away Moneyline Decimal Odds
- Home Moneyline Decimal Odds

You'll find these in columns A through L of the spreadsheet.[3] Once we have these columns formatted, we can begin calculating our various benchmark metrics for the pointspread, total and moneyline.

A	B	C	D	E	F	G
Away Pts	Home Pts	Total Close	Total Actual	Home MOV Actual	Home Win	Away ML US
104	117	209.5	221	-13	1	210
112	114	199	226	-2	1	-205
107	98	198.5	205	9	0	-290
95	89	208	184	6	0	215
123	114	218	237	9	0	-360
94	98	213.5	192	-4	1	115
82	90	217.5	172	-8	1	385
101	89	206	190	12	0	-275
115	103	210.5	218	12	0	150
91	101	231	192	-10	1	290
111	118	199	229	-7	1	-120
119	127	232.5	246	-8	1	1400
98	109	214	207	-11	1	170

STEP 3: CALCULATE RAW ACCURACY

Let's start our benchmark calculations with raw accuracy - what percentage of the time did the market moneyline favourite win the game?

We begin by calculating the no-vig implied probabilities for the home team using the following formula:

=((1/L2)/((1/L2)+(1/K2)))

You'll see that I have completed this step in column P.[4] Next, in column Q we make a raw classification guess where we predict that any probability value in column P over 50% [0.5] is a win [1]. In column R, we grade classification successes. If a home win was predicted and the home team did win, we grade the value as a success [1], otherwise it's a zero. Finally, in Cell N3, we count the number of successes and divide them by the number of trials using the following formula:

```
=COUNTIF(R2:R2745,1)/COUNT(R2:R2745)
```

This gives our dataset a raw classification accuracy score of 68.04%. In other words, 68.04% of the time, the moneyline favourite at this particular book won the game.

N	O	P	Q	R
Market Benchmarks		Home No Vig Probability	Raw classification	Classification Success
Raw Accuracy	ML Log Loss	69.13%	1	1
68.04%	0.5931	35.11%	0	0
ATS RMSE	ATS MAE	28.95%	0	1
13.02	10.08	69.58%	1	0
Total RMSE	Total MAE	24.44%	0	1
17.54	13.93	55.26%	1	1
		80.08%	1	1
		29.56%	0	1
		61.15%	1	0
		75.27%	1	1
		47.83%	0	0
		93.56%	1	1
		64.29%	1	1
		35.71%	0	0

STEP 4: CALCULATE RMSE & MAE

In columns S and T, you'll see we have error calculations for both the pointspread and the total betting lines. These calculations are simply the observed result minus the expected result/market line. We can then use these error calculations to derive both the RMSE and the MAE of each market, which are helpful error metrics we can use to gauge the utility of our models.

In Cells N5 and N7 the RMSE of the pointspread and total markets has been calculated using the formulas:

```
=SQRT(SUMSQ(S2:S2745)/COUNTA(S2:S2745)

=SQRT(SUMSQ(T2:T2745)/COUNTA(T2:T2745)
```

This gives us an RMSE of 13.02 for the closing pointspread and 17.54 for the total. In Cells O5 and O7 the MAE of the pointspread and total markets has been calculated using the formulas:

```
=SUMPRODUCT(ABS(S2:S2745))/COUNT(S2:S2745)
=SUMPRODUCT(ABS(T2:T2745))/COUNT(T2:T2745)
```

This produces an MAE of 10.08 for the pointspread and 13.93 for the total. Ideally, we'd like to create a model that can beat or keep pace with these MAE numbers. These are the key benchmarks we'll want to pay attention to as we move forward.

STEP 5: CALCULATE LOG LOSS

Log Loss is helpful for telling us how accurate the probabilistic moneyline market is in a given sport. We begin by calculating the log error, as shown in column U. This calculation uses the formula:

```
=F2*LN(P2)+(1-F2)*LN(1-P2)
```

Then in Cell O3 we produce the log loss metric using the formula:

```
=SUM(U2:U2745)*-1/COUNT(U2:U2745)
```

This gives us a moneyline market log loss of 0.5931. While this doesn't tell us much on it's own, we can later use it to compare with our models to see if we're on the right track.

At this point, ignoring RMSE for the time being, we have the following target benchmarks for our modelling process:

M	N	O
	Market Benchmarks	
	Raw Accuracy	ML Log Loss
	68.04%	0.5931
	ATS RMSE	ATS MAE
	13.02	10.08
	Total RMSE	Total MAE
	17.54	13.93

- Raw Accuracy: 68.04%
- Pointspread MAE: 10.08
- Total MAE: 13.93
- Moneyline Log Loss: 0.5931

We now have some goals to focus on. If we beat these numbers in any meaningful sense it might be time to consider a model backtest for profitability, and/or placing a series of wagers. If we can't at least keep pace with these benchmarks, we are unlikely to be successful and there is little point risking money to confirm this. Starting with this in mind can save you both time and bankroll units.

Having found our target modelling benchmarks, we can now take these numbers and attempt to beat them by creating a model of our own.

---

1. It's not necessarily mandatory that we beat these metrics. We may be able to have some success with aggressive game filtering if we are able to roughly match the accuracy of the market as well.
2. We might also consider getting this information from a paid source like Indatabet.
3. Unfortunately, there isn't much magic to accomplishing this task in Excel. Data wrangling takes time, and is a very important part of the process.
4. This is a very basic vig removal technique. Other techniques like the logarithmic method mentioned in the first volume of Statistical Sports Models in Excel might also be worth considering here.

2

ELO MODELS: A STARTING POINT

Elo rating models come to us from the world of chess, and have become somewhat ubiquitous in the sports modelling world in the last few years.

It's not hard to see why - they offer a number of benefits and usually serve as a reasonable starting point for your modelling efforts. Specifically, Elo has a number of obvious advantages over the previous paired comparison team based models we've looked at in SSME1.[1]

These benefits include:

- The ability to start with a prior strength rating
- Team strength weighting over time accounted for
- Simple to make, run & test out of sample

There are also a few drawbacks. Elo was created to rate individual chess players in an environment where player skill and results are strongly correlated. There isn't a tremendous amount of noise in chess game results, and as such the applicability of Elo in statistically noisier sports settings might not be particularly high. Additionally, like all team based models, it's hard to factor injuries and lineup changes into an Elo model.[2] That being said, it's a decent place to start as a preliminary modelling attempt. With our freshly calculated NBA target metrics from the last chapter, we can now run a simple Elo model and quickly get a sense of where we're at relative to the betting market.

Can an Elo model beat our target benchmarks? Let's find out.

BASIC ELO FUNCTION

Let's open the "Elo NBA" file and look at the "Elo Mechanics" sheet to get started.

In a standard Elo rating model, the difference between the ratings of two teams is used to calculate the expected win probabilities of a future game. Teams trade "skill points" based on whether they win or lose, and teams that outperform their skill expectation gain more skill points from an upset win than teams heavily favoured to win. The number of skill points available to be traded is denoted by what's known as the K parameter,[3] and win probabilities are calculated using a relatively simple logistic function.

Let's walk through an example.

Suppose at the start of the season the Detroit Pistons and the Chicago Bulls both have Elo ratings of 1500. We can estimate Detroit's chance of winning a game against Chicago using the Elo logistic function:

=1/(1+10^((Chicago Rating - Detroit Rating)/400)

=1/(1+10^((1500-1500)/400)

= 50.00%

With with both teams being equally rated (and ignoring home court advantage), Detroit is unsurprisingly expected to win 50% of the time.

After the game is complete, each team rating will be updated using the K parameter. K is usually set somewhere between 4 and 32, depending on the sport. Games are graded as a [1] for a win, [0] for a loss and [0.5] for a tie. If Detroit wins this game (and Chicago loses), here is how we adjust the ratings when the K parameter is 32:

DET = (Original Rating) + (K parameter) * (Result - Expectation)

= (1500) + (32) * (1 - 0.5)

= **1516**

CHI = (Original Rating) + (K parameter) * (Result - Expectation)

= (1500) + (32) * (0 - 0.5)

= **1484**

So in this instance, Detroit gains 16 skill points because they exceeded their performance expectation by 50% and (0.5 * 32) = 16. Vice versa for Chicago. If these two teams were then immediately scheduled to play each other again, Detroit's updated win probability would be:

= 1/(1+10^((1484-1516)/400))

= **54.59%**

That's the basic idea behind Elo. If you want to explore the conceptual functioning in more detail, you can see how rating changes occur between teams in the "Elo Mechanics" sheet. You can adjust the win/loss results and the K parameter to observe how the rating adjustments change, which should hopefully assist your understanding of how Elo works.

A	B	C	D	E	F	G	H	I
Game #	Team	Original Rating	Elo Logistic Function	Result	Rating Adjust		K Parameter	32
1	Detroit	1500	50.00%	1	1516			
	Chicago	1500	50.00%	0	1484			
Game #	Team	Original Rating	Elo Logistic Function	Result	Rating Adjust			
2	Detroit	1516	54.59%	1	1531			
	Chicago	1484	45.41%	0	1469			
Game #	Team	Original Rating	Elo Logistic Function	Result	Rating Adjust			
3	Detroit	1531	58.70%					
	Chicago	1469	41.30%					

However there are few added touches needed to make this model work well. First, we need to tune the K parameter for the sport we're trying to model. Next, we must account for home court advantage, and lastly we should look to improve the starting Elo ratings of each team to help guide the model early in the season.

SETTING THE K PARAMETER

The optimal K parameter varies by sport and even by league. The higher the K, the more information we think each game result tells us about underlying team strength. Here are some general K parameter suggestions based on different sports:

Basketball: ~20

Baseball: ~4

Hockey: ~8

Soccer: ~18

Football: ~20

You'll want to conduct your own testing of course, but these numbers should help get you started. It takes a little tinkering to get it just right, but Solver in Excel can help you find the optimal value. Simply set Solver's target to minimize one of our error metrics (MAE, log loss, etc.) and select the K parameter on the sheet in Cell B1 as the variable cell to change.

HOME COURT ADVANTAGE

Home court advantage [HCA] in the NBA varies between approximately 2.7 and 3.5 points, so for this model we'll move forward on the basis that it's approximately 2.8 points. We need a way to add this into the model in order to more accurately forecast each game. The simplest way to do this is to calculate a quantity of Elo skill points that roughly corresponds to the additional win percentage teams have when playing at home. We can then add these Elo points to a home team's Elo rating when using the logistic function to forecast game win probabilities.

To do this we must first convert HCA into an implied win percentage. As the relationship between spreads and win percentages is generally considered to be a logistic curve, we can use the following equation:

=EXP(Spread * X)/(1 + EXP(Spread * X))

Where "Spread" is our -2.8 points of home advantage, and "X" is a number determined by running a logistic regression on a large dataset containing pointspreads and win/loss outcomes for the NBA.[4] The proper value for "X" appears to vary between -0.132 and -0.157, so using -0.132 as our "X" value, the corresponding win percentage to our -2.8 point HCA is:

=EXP(-2.8*(-0.132))/(1 + EXP(-2.8 *(-0.132)))

= **59.14%**

Now that we have converted our HCA spread to an implied win percentage, we need to find the corresponding number of Elo skill points that would produce a home win probability of ~59.14% between two evenly matched teams. This can be accomplished by using Excel's Solver function on the "HCA" sheet inside the Elo NBA Excel file. We set the target Cell to "D3", the objective to "Value of 0.5914", by changing Cells "E2". We then click "Solve" and Excel will calculate the optimal value of Elo skill points for our HCA.

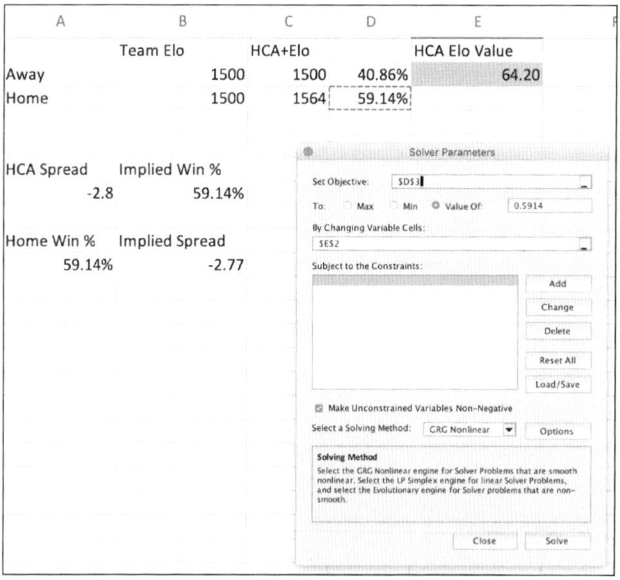

After Solver completes the calculation, we can see that ~64.2 Elo skill points is a good fit. We can then take this value and add it to a home team's Elo rating when we run the Elo logistic function. Going back to our Detroit vs. Chicago example from earlier, our new Elo logistic function works like this when Detroit is playing at home:

=1/(1+10^((Chicago Rating - (Detroit Rating+ HCA Elo Pts))/400)

=1/(1+10^((1500-(1500+64.2))/400)

= 59.14%

Converting this number back to a spread is also relatively straightforward. We can take the home team's expected win percentage for this game, extrapolate season wins from it, and then divide wins above average by 2.7.[5] Since Detroit in the above matchup is favoured to win 59.14% of the time:

Estimated Spread = (((59.14% * 82 Games) - 41 Games)/-2.7)

Detroit Estimated Spread = -2.77, or about -2.8 points.

TUNING STARTING RATINGS WITH SEASON WIN TOTALS

Elo models typically start out with every team having a rating of 1500, which could be considered an "uninformed prior". By giving every team the same starting rating, we're effectively saying that we have no way to differentiate the teams' respective strengths before observing the first game result. This is of course not totally true - even before the first tip off, we have *some* idea of which teams should be better than others.

One way to incorporate this information into an Elo model to help boost its accuracy is to use the season win totals market to estimate starting Elo ratings. This can point the model in the right direction from the outset of the season, and hopefully means that it will require less game result data to begin tracking team strengths reasonably. Essentially, there is no good reason why a team projected to win 50 games should have the same starting rating as a team projected to win 28.

Let's start by getting all the game result data from the 2018-2019 season (the previous season) from basketball-reference.com and then running the Elo model with starting ratings of 1500 for each team. This has been completed in the "2018 Previous Season" sheet. After running the entire previous season through the model, we will have ending Elo ratings for every team, and we will also have end of season win totals as well. You'll find these in columns AZ and BC of the "2018 Previous Season" sheet.

AY	AZ	BA	BB	BC
TEAM	End of Season Elo	Final SRS	Final Win%	Final Wins
Atlanta Hawks	1435.72	-6.1	35.40%	29
Boston Celtics	1572.78	4.4	59.80%	49
Brooklyn Nets	1548.34	-0.1	51.20%	42
Charlotte Hornets	1516.30	-1.1	47.60%	39
Chicago Bulls	1315.73	-8.5	26.80%	22
Cleveland Cavaliers	1296.23	-9.6	23.20%	19
Dallas Mavericks	1396.18	-1.2	40.20%	33
Denver Nuggets	1606.96	4	65.90%	54

We can then make a simple regression using Elo ratings as the Y variable and total wins as the X variable. This essentially asks the question "given a season win total of X, what should the Elo rating be?". This has been completed in the "Starting Elo Regression" sheet. We end up with a regression equation that looks more or less like this:

Starting Elo Rating = 1103.962 + ((Win Total) * 9.660)

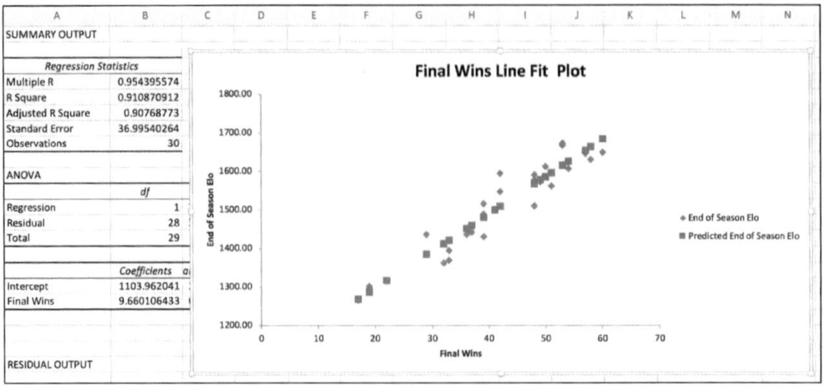

We can then take this formula and combine it with the season win total market projections for the 2019-2020 season and estimate the starting Elo rating for each team. For example, if the Detroit Pistons have a season win total line of 37.5, then their starting Elo rating in this model should be:

Detroit = 1103.962 + 9.660 * (37.5 Projected Wins)

Starting Elo = **1466.22**

It clearly won't be perfect, but it will be much better than simply starting every team at 1500. You'll see these estimated starting Elo ratings have been inputted into the "2019 Current Season" sheet for each team in row 2.

RUNNING THE MODEL

Now that we've gone over all the various components of this Elo model, let's walkthrough how to use it. Open up the "2019 Current Season" sheet. You'll see that the game result data is inputted into columns A, B, C and D. Starting estimated Elo ratings from our regression against the previous season have been inputted for each team in row 2. New game observations are added to the bottom of the dataset, in chronological order. Once you've inputted the game data into the first four columns, you next have to select and drag down/populate the result functions and Elo rating update functions for each team, which are found in columns E through AK. Column E is the Elo logistic function that produces a home win probability forecast for the game information contained in its corresponding row. Columns F & G are the result columns where a "1" for either the home or away team denotes a win, and a 0 denotes a loss.

VLOOKUP × ✓ fx =1/(1+10^((LOOKUP($C3,$H$1:$AK$1,$H2:$AK2)-(LOOKUP($A3,$H$1:$AK$1,$H2:$AK2)+$E$1))/400))

	A	B	C	D	E
1	K Parameter	32	Home Court Advantage		64.2
2	Home Team	Home Score	Away Team	Away Score	Home Team Estimated Win %
3	Los Angeles Clippers	112	Los Angeles Lakers	102	=1/(1+10^((LOOKUP($C3,$H$1:$AK$
4	Toronto Raptors	130	New Orleans Pelicans	122	68.11%
5	Brooklyn Nets	126	Minnesota Timberwolves	127	71.62%
6	Charlotte Hornets	126	Chicago Bulls	125	46.73%
7	Dallas Mavericks	108	Washington Wizards	100	73.82%
8	Indiana Pacers	110	Detroit Pistons	119	70.48%
9	Miami Heat	120	Memphis Grizzlies	101	77.89%
10	Orlando Magic	94	Cleveland Cavaliers	85	78.83%
11	Philadelphia 76ers	107	Boston Celtics	93	66.89%
12	Phoenix Suns	124	Sacramento Kings	95	46.73%
13	Portland Trail Blazers	100	Denver Nuggets	108	50.90%

The out of sample error calculations for the model are found in columns AN to AW. These perform the calculations we used in the first chapter to create our target benchmarks, and the resulting model performance can be found in column AM. If these numbers look better than our target benchmarks (higher accuracy or smaller error metrics), it is a positive sign.

AL	AM	AN	AO	AP
	Model Benchmarks	Home Elo Rating	Away Elo Rating	Home Est Win%
	Raw Accuracy	1695	1601	63.10%
	67.24%	1617	1486	68.11%
	Spread MAE 1	1608	1447	71.62%
	9.96	1395	1418	46.73%
	Log Loss	1559	1379	73.82%
	0.6028	1617	1466	70.48%
		1588	1370	77.89%
	Total Games	1569	1341	78.83%
	818	1695	1572	66.89%
	Games Correct	1443	1466	46.73%
	550	1617	1611	50.90%
		1617	1360	81.48%

Current team Elo ratings as of the most recent game (the bottom row in the current dataset) are shown in column AZ. Finally, game predictions can be made using the Cells starting at BD3.

AX	AY	AZ	BA	BB	BC	BD	BE
	TEAM	Current Team Elo Rating	Rank		Predictions	Team	Elo Rating
	Atlanta Hawks	1363.31	24		Away	Detroit Pistons	1311.20
	Boston Celtics	1651.64	6		Home	Chicago Bulls	1362.76
	Brooklyn Nets	1492.87	17				
	Charlotte Hornets	1336.65	26				
	Chicago Bulls	1362.76	25				
	Cleveland Cavaliers	1266.74	30				
	Dallas Mavericks	1546.43	13				
	Denver Nuggets	1652.25	5				
	Detroit Pistons	1311.20	27				
	Golden State Warriors	1305.50	28				

MAKING GAME PREDICTIONS

In columns BC, BD, BE, BF and BG of the "2019 Current Season" sheet you can see the game prediction function. To forecast an upcoming game using the current dataset, input the team names into Cells BD3 and BD4. The sheet will use Excel's VLOOKUP function to find the current team Elo ratings from column AZ, run the Elo logistic function and then calculate a pointspread estimate. From there, you can convert the win probabilities into prices and compare the forecasted spread to current market lines. Before you do that however, it's important to be cognizant of whether the model appears to be outperforming the market competition (see below).

BC	BD	BE	BF	BG
Predictions	Team	Elo Rating	Elo Logistic Function	Spread Estimate
Away	Detroit Pistons	1311.20	33.93%	4.88
Home	Chicago Bulls	1362.76	66.07%	-4.88

COMPARING MODEL BENCHMARKS

So after running our Elo model and tinkering with it, how did it do? We can see our model's out of sample results in column AM of the "2019 Current Season" sheet:

AL	AM	AN	AO
	Model Benchmarks	Home Elo Rating	Away Elo Rating
	Raw Accuracy	1695	1601
	67.24%	1617	1486
	Spread MAE 1	1608	1447
	9.96	1395	1418
	Log Loss	1559	1379
	0.6028	1617	1466
		1588	1370
	Total Games	1569	1341
	818	1695	1572
	Games Correct	1443	1466
	550	1617	1611
		1617	1360

- Raw Accuracy: 67.24%
- Pointspread MAE: 9.96 (not bad!)
- Log Loss: 0.6028

Overall, not great. Our Elo model appears to have a minuscule advantage in MAE, but is otherwise falling short of the market's target benchmarks from chapter 1.

It's been a fun model building exercise, but it looks like Elo isn't going to deliver positive expected value for us on it's own in the NBA. To take the next step forward, we'll need to drill down beyond team based approaches and start to account for individual player performance. However, before we do that, we should probably talk about predictive statistics and some approaches that can be used for uncovering the kind of data that will maximize our chances of success.

E	F	G
64.2		
Home Team Estimated Win %	Home Result	Away Result
63.10%	=IF(B3>D3,1,IF(D3=B3,0.5,0))	
68.11%	1	0
71.62%	0	1
46.73%	1	0
73.82%	1	0

This model framework can be applied to most sports. You simply have to do a bit of legwork to calculate home field advantage and spread/win % conversion. You'll also want to experiment with finding the optimal K parameter (using Solver to minimize the model MAE while adjusting the K parameter). If you're looking to apply it to a trinomial outcome sport like soccer, you'll also need to adjust the result columns F & G to account for the possibility of a draw (suggested IF function pictured above), but otherwise it should be fairly straightforward to apply to your preferred sport. Finally, I have included additional Elo model files for the NHL, NFL and the English Premier League in the download package. Feel free to experiment with them if you'd like.

---

1. Statistical Sports Models in Excel Volume 1. [SSME1]
2. It's certainly possible to do of course. Creating an Elo rating for every player and then using some form of weighted sum to derive a team rating is something worth investigating.

3. Finding the appropriate K parameter is the subject of some debate. Set it too high and individual games drastically affect team ratings. Set it too low and changes in team strength are accounted for too slowly. Testing is required to get it just right. Fivethirtyeight uses a K parameter of 20 for the NBA. Using the model shown, I found a decent fit with a K parameter of ~32.
4. Michael Shackleford of WizardofOdds.com found "X" to be -0.16, but my recent tests have indicated it might be slightly less than that. You can see the logistic curve for this relationship plotted using different "X" values in the "HCA" sheet of the Elo NBA file in columns H, I and J.
5. You'll have to find this number for your respective sport to use this method for a different market. In the NBA, every additional 2.7 wins above average equates roughly to 1 additional point of MOV strength.

3

HOW PREDICTIVE IS STAT X?

Statistical modelling is simply a tool, much like a measuring tape or a carpenter's level. It's certainly a powerful tool, but like all tools, it can be misused or applied in a way that does more harm than good. This is especially true when attempting to uncover causal or predictive relationships in data. As the saying goes, *"a little knowledge can be a dangerous thing"*.

For example, it's almost impossible to go through an entire NFL season without hearing at least one head coach say something along the lines of: *"our team wins more when we run the ball more often."*

This is of course not necessarily true.

Teams that are winning naturally want to run out the remaining game clock, resulting in run plays being called more often. That doesn't necessarily mean that running the ball *causes* winning. It is correlated, but not necessarily causative.

This is a common pitfall in modelling work. It's easy for a beginner to mistake a relationship they've found between two variables as causal and erroneously draw the wrong conclusion. In this chapter, I'd like to give you some guidance on how to avoid making this mistake by following a process to uncover potentially useful predictive variables.

The question is simple: how do we determine the predictive power of stat X? Let's start by quickly discussing the difference between predictive and descriptive statistics. From there we'll walkthrough a basic 3-step process for testing the forecasting power of a given stat. In keeping with the NBA theme from the first two chapters, I'll use "Offensive Box Plus/Minus" [OBPM] from Basketball-Reference.com as our "stat X".[1]

DESCRIPTIVE VS PREDICTIVE STATISTICS

The field of statistics is generally used for two broad purposes: to explain relationships in data and to forecast future occurrences using relationships in data. While these two purposes share some overlap, they are not the same. When building a sports model for the purposes of betting, we obviously care much more about what will happen in the future than describing what has already occurred.

While descriptive models and statistics can have *some* predictive power, they are generally relaying information about what has already happened and can therefore be considered "backwards looking". An example of this would be a team's season win percentage. It has some predictive power, but is largely describing what has already occurred rather than giving us a clear indication of future performance. This is contrasted by a predictive model or statistic, which ideally is optimized to be "forward looking", or more indicative of future occurrences than past ones. When looking for this type of predictive variable, we generally want to see three things in our testing process: a strong in-sample correlation between the variable in question and our target variable, evidence of repeatability and strong out of sample correlation.

Let's go over each of these now. Open the "Predictive Stats" Excel file to follow along with the rest of this chapter.

A	B	C	D	E	F
In-Sample Correlation	71.71%				
Split Test Correlation	68.14%				
Out-Sample Correlation	54.54%				
Player	2017 OBPM	2018 MP	2018 PTS	2018 PPM	2018 OBPM
Steven Adams	2.2	2669	1108	0.415136755	0.6
Bam Adebayo	-1.6	1913	729	0.381076843	-0.6
LaMarcus Aldridge	3	2687	1727	0.642724228	1.2
Jarrett Allen	-1.3	2096	873	0.416507634	-0.7
Al-Farouq Aminu	-0.8	2292	760	0.331588133	0.1
Kyle Anderson	-0.3	1281	346	0.270101483	-2.1
Giannis Antetokounmpo	3.9	2358	1994	0.845631891	5.7
OG Anunoby	0.2	1352	469	0.346893491	-1.3
Ryan Arcidiacono	-3.3	1961	544	0.277409485	-0.1

STEP 1: IN-SAMPLE CORRELATION

Let's suppose that we're interested in predicting future NBA player points per minute [PPM]. If we can find a statistic that will help us to do this, we might be able to create a player based model that will allow us to more accurately forecast future basketball games. We suspect that OBPM might be a useful input variable to help us predict PPM, so we're going to test it to find out.

The first step is to test in-sample correlation between OBPM and PPM from the same season, using the correlation function in the Data Analysis Toolpack in Excel or the CORREL function. On the sheet in columns E and F I've imported player data from Basketball-Reference.com for PPM and OBPM and then filtered out players with less than 1,000 minutes played in the 2018-2019 season. Then, using the CORREL function in Cell B1, I input the following Excel command:

```
=CORREL(F5:F258,E5:E258)
```

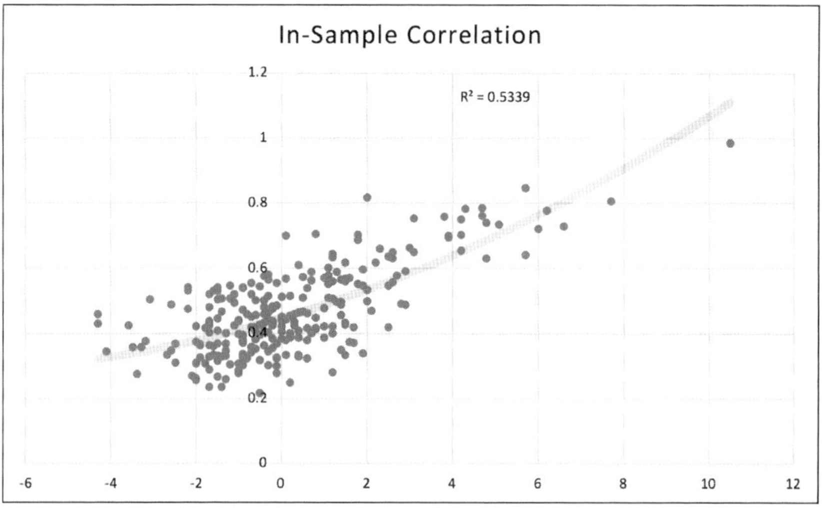

We can see that the in-sample correlation between PPM and OBPM during the same season is 71.71%, with an R-Squared value of 53.39%. That's a pretty strong positive relationship, so there is no reason not to continue with our next tests. Incidentally, a slightly curved polynomial trend line appears to be a better fit than a linear one. With a strong in-sample correlation found, we can proceed to testing OBPM's repeatability through a split half test. Many beginner modellers run this in-sample correlation test and then proceed on that basis alone, which I would suggest is a suboptimal approach. The next two steps are very important.

STEP 2: SPLIT-HALF TEST

The second step is to test OBPM for repeatability or stability. We want to try and model performance that is related to skill rather than randomness (noise). If the processes underlying OBPM are repeatable, then it's possible OBPM is connected to player skill. If there is low repeatability for a player's OBPM from season to season or even between the first and second half of the same season, then it might not be an overly helpful statistic to include in a future model. One example of this would be turnovers. While they might be strongly correlated with game outcomes in-sample, a split half test would likely reveal that they are essentially random with low repeatability. Naturally, we're looking to discard potential model inputs that suggest low repeatability.

To make use of the split half test for repeatability we divide up a statistic between the first and second half of a season, between odd and even games from the same season, or even between two separate seasons and then check the correlation between the two samples. Higher correlation between the samples indicates higher repeatability. On the sheet in Cell B2, you'll see I've completed this step, testing the correlation between 2017 OBPM and 2018 OBPM for each player in the dataset:

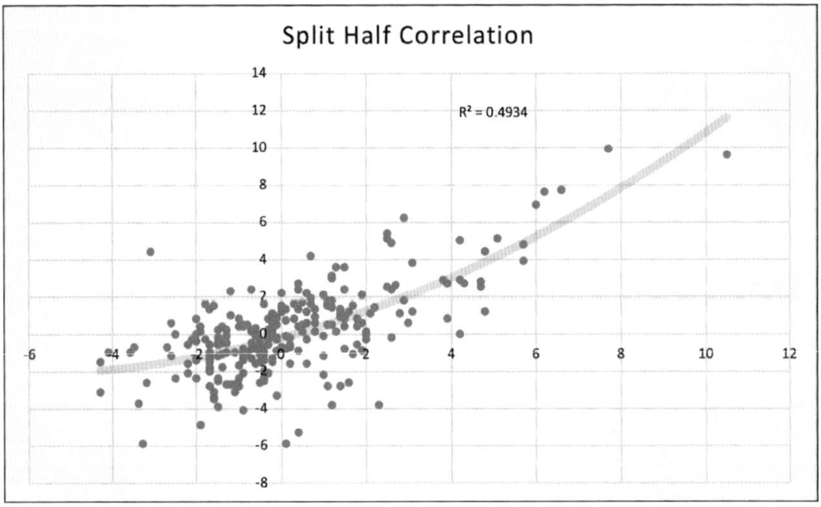

While our correlation isn't quite as strong as the first test, we still have a decent positive relationship between OBPM in 2017 and 2018 at 68.14% (and an R-Squared value of 49.34%). This suggests that OBPM *might* be mapping a repeatable process related to player skill - which is obviously one of the indicators we're looking for.

STEP 3: OUT-SAMPLE CORRELATION

The final step is to test 2017 OBPM for out of sample correlation with our target variable, 2018 PPM. If a player's previous season OBPM is reasonably correlated with a future out of sample season PPM performance, then this is a solid indication that OBPM may be useful as a predictive model input. In Cell B3 you'll see that I've used the CORREL function again to test the correlation between 2017 OBPM and 2018 PPM.

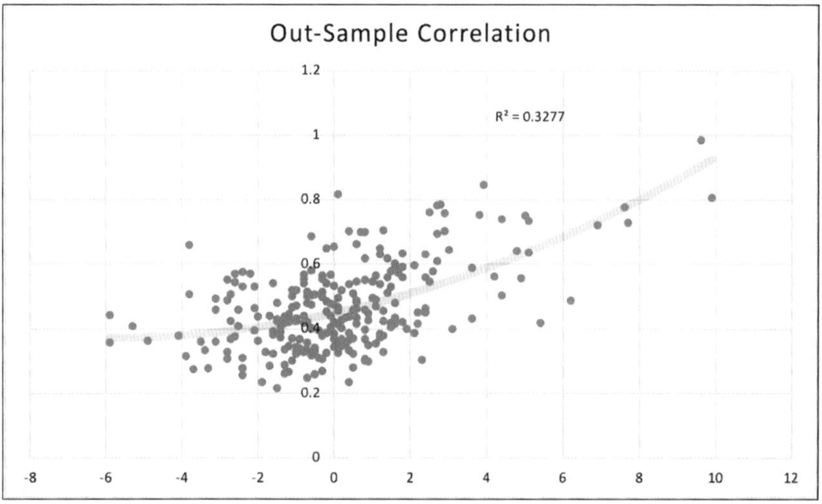

While this test returns our lowest values yet at 54.54% correlation and 32.77% R-Squared, these are still potentially promising numbers. Every sport environment will be slightly different due to varied levels of inherent randomness, but based on these three tests OBPM is at least worth testing out as a predictive input in a player based model going forward.

In actual practice, you're usually going to want to test many different variables at the same time to speed up the process and compare potential candidate inputs with one another. You're also going to want to use a larger sample size than what's been shown here if possible. However, this basic 3 part testing procedure will help you to avoid using variables in your modelling efforts that have questionable predictive value. As always, domain knowledge about the sport you're modelling should be used to guide your statistical search efforts. You might also consider learning more about the advanced stats in your preferred sport to generate ideas about where to look for potentially predictive data relationships.

---

1. It's important to remember that OBPM was intended to be a descriptive statistic that assigns credit to a player for their box score contributions. Some of these types of single player statistics are certainly better than others for predictive power, and all of them struggle to really capture a player's contribution to defense. That being said, OBPM should serve as a decent example for this predictive stat test process even if it is removed from the contextual comparison of other competing box score metrics.

PLAYER BASED MODELS

4

NBA WIN SHARES MODEL

Win shares in the NBA aren't overly predictive, but do have some measure of forecasting power. This model uses win shares per minute and expected player minutes to estimate the pointspread and win probabilities of a game. It also serves as a basic introduction to combining player inputs into an Excel based model.

Let's open up the "NBA Win Shares" Excel file and begin.

When you open the file, you'll see that we're using an example game from January 18th, 2020 when the Detroit Pistons were on the road playing the Atlanta Hawks. All of the player names for each team's starting 10 lineup (5 starters and 5 bench players) are entered into column A. Exact spelling is important as VLOOKUP will fail to find the appropriate player data if you're missing an accent over a letter (Ante Žižić comes to mind here). If you type in a player's name and get any errors in the data retrieval, simply go to sheets 2 or 3 and look for the specific spelling, then copy and paste from there.

A	B	C	D	E
AWAY STARTERS	POSITION	% MIN	ADJ MIN	WIN SHARES /48*MIN
Bruce Brown	SG	11.50%	29.50	0.036
Derrick Rose	PG	10.59%	27.17	0.061
Tony Snell	SF	10.91%	28.01	0.044
Sekou Doumbouya	SF	6.57%	16.86	0.014
Andre Drummond	C	14.08%	36.13	0.096
AWAY BENCH	POSITION	% MIN	ADJ MIN	WIN SHARES /48*MIN
Sviatoslav Mykhailiuk	SF	8.30%	21.29	0.017
Langston Galloway	SG	10.55%	27.08	0.052
Markieff Morris	PF	9.27%	23.79	0.022
Christian Wood	PF	7.01%	18.00	0.065
Thon Maker	C	4.74%	12.16	0.020
	MIN SUM	93.52%	240.00	34.94
HOME STARTERS	POSITION	% MIN	ADJ MIN	WIN SHARES /48*MIN
Trae Young	PG	14.64%	35.78	0.087
Kevin Huerter	SG	11.38%	27.81	0.029
Cam Reddish	SF	10.74%	26.25	-0.032

Once that is complete, the rest of the sheet makes some calculations to produce a forecast by retrieving each player's position[1], percentage of minutes played and win shares per 48 minutes from two other sheets in the file: "2. Player Advanced Data" and "3. Player Totals Data". You might think of these two sheets as a very simplistic database that we can retrieve player data from using commands in Excel like VLOOKUP and INDEX. The data in both of these sheets comes from player advanced and totals data from Basketball-Reference.com, and can be either copy/pasted into your sheets or automatically imported using Excel's "import from web" function.

A	B	C	D	E	F	G	H	I	J	K
Rk	Player	Pos	Age	Tm	G	MP	PER	TS%	3PAr	FTr
1	Steven Adams	C	26	OKC	36	1017	22.3	0.618	0.003	0.42
2	Bam Adebayo	C	22	MIA	39	1339	20.7	0.629	0.023	0.533
3	LaMarcus Aldridge	C	34	SAS	36	1189	21	0.584	0.177	0.23
4	Nickeil Alexander-Walker	SG	21	NOP	31	423	8.4	0.445	0.539	0.109
5	Grayson Allen	SG	24	MEM	25	423	11.6	0.583	0.533	0.191
6	Jarrett Allen	C	21	BRK	38	1008	21.3	0.669	0.012	0.605
7	Kadeem Allen	SG	27	NYK	7	66	16	0.52	0.345	0.138
8	Al-Farouq Aminu	PF	29	ORL	18	380	7.8	0.395	0.419	0.337

UNDERSTANDING THE CALCULATIONS

The basic idea behind this model is to reduce win shares to a per minute statistic, multiply the win shares per minute by each player's expected minutes, and then sum the team total of win shares to calculate season win totals. Once we calculate an expected season win total for each team and compare them, it's fairly straightforward to calculate an expected pointspread and win probability for each team with their current lineups.

PLAYER MINUTES

In columns C and D you'll see the headings "% MIN" and "ADJ MIN". This is where we generate a very basic player minute estimate using the average percentage of minutes played in a game by each player and then make an adjustment so that the total sum of all player minutes on each team equals 240. Since each team has 5 players on the floor at any given time and a game lasts 48 minutes, all player minutes must fit inside the (5 * 48 = 240) framework, otherwise our projections won't make much sense.

Column C retrieves the average percentage of player minutes using the VLOOKUP command. This is an added variable found in the "3. Player Totals Data" sheet in column AF, and is calculated by dividing individual player minutes played by the total estimated number of available team minutes for all relevant games (number of player games multiplied by 240). This input is retrieved for each player on a team, and then the total is summed in cell C13 and C27 for away and home teams.

You'll notice that these two cells feature percentages that are typically either more or less than 100%, indicating that we need to adjust them proportionally so that the total player minutes for each team equals 240 minutes, or 100%. This is accomplished by dividing the player's minute percentage by the team's summed minute percentage and then multiplying by 240. So if Bruce Brown is expected to get 11.50% of Detroit's minutes, but Detroit's summed minutes percentage is 93.52%, then the correction works as follows:

Bruce Brown Minutes = (11.50%/93.52%) * 240

Bruce Brown Minutes = 29.50

A	B	C	D	E
AWAY STARTERS	POSITION	% MIN	ADJ MIN	WIN SHARES /48*MIN
Bruce Brown	SG	11.50%	=C2/$C$13*240	
Derrick Rose	PG	10.59%	27.17	0.061
Tony Snell	SF	10.91%	28.01	0.044
Sekou Doumbouya	SF	6.57%	16.86	0.014
Andre Drummond	C	14.08%	36.13	0.096
AWAY BENCH	POSITION	% MIN	ADJ MIN	WIN SHARES /48*MIN
Sviatoslav Mykhailiuk	SF	8.30%	21.29	0.017
Langston Galloway	SG	10.55%	27.08	0.052
Markieff Morris	PF	9.27%	23.79	0.022
Christian Wood	PF	7.01%	18.00	0.065
Thon Maker	C	4.74%	12.16	0.020
	MIN SUM	93.52%	240.00	34.94

Doing this for every player on each respective team produces adjusted minute expectations that sum to 240 total minutes. While you can certainly go more in-depth on minute projections than this, it's an approachable place to start.

WIN SHARES PER MINUTE

In column E, the model retrieves each player's win shares per 48 minutes statistic from the "2. Advanced Player Data" sheet. Each cell in this column then multiplies the retrieved win share number by a player's expected minutes and then divides by 48. Once this is complete for all players on a team, the total win shares number is summed and then multiplied by 82 (games) to produce a season total win expectation in cells E13 and E27.

VLOOKUP fx =VLOOKUP(A2,'2. Player Advanced Data'!$B$2:$AC$507,23,FALSE)*D2/48

	A	B	C	D	E	F
1	AWAY STARTERS	POSITION	% MIN	ADJ MIN	WIN SHARES /48*MIN	
2	Bruce Brown	SG	11.50%	29.50	=VLOOKUP(A2,'2. Player Advanced D	
3	Derrick Rose	PG	10.59%	27.17	0.061	Hor
4	Tony Snell	SF	10.91%	28.01	0.044	
5	Sekou Doumbouya	SF	6.57%	16.86	0.014	
6	Andre Drummond	C	14.08%	36.13	0.096	
7	AWAY BENCH	POSITION	% MIN	ADJ MIN	WIN SHARES /48*MIN	
8	Sviatoslav Mykhailiuk	SF	8.30%	21.29	0.017	
9	Langston Galloway	SG	10.55%	27.08	0.052	
10	Markieff Morris	PF	9.27%	23.79	0.022	
11	Christian Wood	PF	7.01%	18.00	0.065	

PRODUCING A GAME FORECAST

In columns I through M you can see the game prediction calculations. Cells I2 and I3 are the season win total estimates we calculated before from cells E13 and E27. We then divide these numbers by 82 in cells J2 and J3 to arrive at a season win percentage for each team.

H	I	J	K	L	M
Team	Expected Season Wins	Expected Season Win %	Transform %	Game Win %	Estimated Spread
Detroit Pistons	34.94	42.61%	30.09%	54.94%	-1.50
Atlanta Hawks	24.10	29.39%	16.87%	45.06%	1.50

In this case, Detroit's win percentage is 42.61% and Atlanta's is 29.39%. In order to compare these two individual team winning percentages, we then transform[2] them as follows:

Detroit =((42.61%*(1-29.39%))

Detroit = 30.09%

Atlanta =((29.39%*(1-42.61%))

Atlanta = 16.87%

We then scale the probabilities so that they sum to 100% and factor in the roughly 9.14% home court advantage:

Detroit = (((30.09%/(30.09%+16.87%))- 9.14%)

Detroit = 54.94%

Atlanta = 45.06% (1-54.94%)

You'll find that these calculations were completed in columns K and L of the main dashboard sheet. The only thing left to do now is convert the win probabilities into an estimated spread using a formula we've seen before in chapter 2:

Detroit = ((54.94% * 82)-41)/-2.7

Detroit = -1.50 / Atlanta = +1.50

From here we can calculate the fair odds for the moneyline and compare our spread estimate to market lines. This particular game started out as a pick 'em and ended up at Detroit -1.5 and 1.85/2.06 on the moneyline (representing a modest 1.64% value on Detroit based on this model). The Pistons had a blowout win here (33 points), but we'd still want to look at a sizeable number of game results and compare our model's metrics to market benchmarks before making any betting decisions. To that end, sheet "4. Model Testing" is provided so that you can copy and paste your game forecasts from the main dashboard in order to track your results. Using the MAE, RMSE and other metrics from chapter 1 will help you to see how the model is performing. In the next chapter, we'll look to expand on what we've built here by using a slightly more complicated process.

---

1. The player position data is purely for your own information in this model. It doesn't factor into the forecast calculations.
2. This will look familiar to you if you've read Joe Peta's "Trading Bases" at page 70.

5

NBA BOX SCORE PLUS/MINUS MODEL

How might we improve on the win shares model from the last chapter?

One possibility is to pick a slightly more predictive input variable, so let's try that here with Basketball-Reference.com's Box Plus/Minus [BPM] statistic. Tests conducted by members of the basketball analytics community have shown that while win shares have some predictive power, you can do much better with an advanced box score metric like BPM, PIPM or RAPM if you're attempting to predict player performance.[1]

This type of metric in basketball attempts to credit players for their personal box score contributions using various methodologies to weight the underlying components. Reducing player contributions to a single number creates challenges with accounting for defensive contributions and roster changes, but overall a model input variable like BPM should be an improvement over win shares.

Let's give it a shot. To make it easier to compare with our win shares model from the previous chapter, we'll use the same game example and see what our new BPM model thinks about Detroit's chances against Atlanta. The general structure of the model will be very similar to our previous attempt, except that we'll have to incorporate a few additional steps to account for the fact that BPM is a "per 100 possessions" based statistic.

UNDERSTANDING BOX PLUS/MINUS [BPM]

According to the basketball-reference.com website, BPM is *"a box score estimate of the points per 100 possessions a player contributed above a league-average player, translated to an average team"*. Looking at the formula for how BPM is constructed[2] we can see that we will have to transform it a bit in order to extract what we really want, which is BPM *per minute*. We should then be able to take this BPM per minute variable and multiply it by expected player minutes to produce a game forecast using the specific lineups that each team will put on the floor.

Let's open up the "NBA BPM" Excel file and take a look.

A	B	C	D	E	F
AWAY STARTERS	POSITION	% MIN	ADJ MIN	Possessions/Min	Expected Possessions
Bruce Brown	SG	11.50%	29.50	0.335	9.891
Derrick Rose	PG	10.59%	27.17	0.717	19.483
Tony Snell	SF	10.91%	28.01	0.270	7.575
Sekou Doumbouya	SF	6.57%	16.86	0.379	6.385
Andre Drummond	C	14.08%	36.13	0.411	14.856
AWAY BENCH	POSITION	% MIN	ADJ MIN	Possessions/Min	Expected Possessions
Sviatoslav Mykhailiuk	SF	8.30%	21.29	0.361	7.687
Langston Galloway	SG	10.55%	27.08	0.367	9.939
Markieff Morris	PF	9.27%	23.79	0.467	11.105
Christian Wood	PF	7.01%	18.00	0.390	7.015
Thon Maker	C	4.74%	12.16	0.262	3.181
	MIN SUM	93.52%	240.00		105.36

You'll notice that the basic structure of the sheets is very similar to our previous win shares model, except that we have some additional model inputs and calculations. The "database sheets" and VLOOKUP data retrieving functions work similarly to our previous model, as does the static "Model Testing" sheet. In column A once again we input the specific players that we expect to play for each team starting with the away team up top in rows 2 to 12. This incorporates 10 players from each team. While it's true that some teams feature a lineup rotation that includes 11 or 12+ players, factoring 10 players covers the bulk of expected team strength variation.

Columns B, C and D are the same as our previous model and serve to retrieve player position data and minute expectations. Columns E through I are however new and require some additional explanation.

B	C	D	E	F	G	H	I
POSITION	% MIN	ADJ MIN	Possessions/Min	Expected Possessions	On Court % ADJ	BPM/Min	Spread Value
SG	11.50%	29.50	0.335	9.891	64.75	-0.01	-0.270
PG	10.59%	27.17	0.717	19.483	59.64	0.01	0.199
SF	10.91%	28.01	0.270	7.575	61.48	-0.02	-0.564
SF	6.57%	16.86	0.379	6.385	37.01	-0.10	-1.666
C	14.08%	36.13	0.411	14.856	79.31	0.05	1.983
POSITION	% MIN	ADJ MIN	Possessions/Min	Expected Possessions	On Court % ADJ	BPM/Min	Spread Value
SF	8.30%	21.29	0.361	7.687	46.74	-0.05	-0.974
SG	10.55%	27.08	0.367	9.939	59.44	-0.01	-0.248
PF	9.27%	23.79	0.467	11.105	52.22	-0.04	-0.957
PF	7.01%	18.00	0.390	7.015	39.51	0.01	0.099
C	4.74%	12.16	0.262	3.181	26.68	-0.03	-0.311
MIN SUM	93.52%	240.00		105.36		-0.18	-2.71

CALCULATING BPM PER MINUTE

Since BPM is a possession based metric, we need to estimate player possessions and team possessions in order to reduce BPM to a per minute rate that will be useful to our model. We start by estimating player possessions, then sum these values to estimate team possessions, and then finally weight the possessions to determine how much influence on the game each player's BPM will be expected to have. This produces an estimated spread value for each player in the lineup.

Here's how we do it:

STEP 1: CALCULATE PLAYER POSSESSIONS

In the "3. Player Totals Data" sheet, you'll see that there are two new constructed variables: Estimated Possessions in column AG and Possessions Per Minute in column AH. Estimated Possessions are the estimated total possessions a player has had during the season and are calculated using the following formula (which I've found to be slightly more accurate than other existing formulas you may have encountered before):

= -2.23 + (1.07*FGA) + (0.37*FTA) + (-1.23*ORB) + (0.87*TOV)

Here are the regression variables:

FGA: Field goal attempts

FTA: Free throw attempts

ORB: Offensive rebounds

TOV: Turnovers

This produces a total possession estimate for every player in the league in column AG. In column AH, we simply divide the value in column AG by the number of total minutes played by each player to arrive at possessions per minute.

AF	AG	AH
% MIN	Estimated Possessions	Possessions/Min
11.77%	=-2.23+(1.07*J2)+(0.37*T2)+(-1.23*V2)+(0.87*AB2)	
14.31%	474.77	0.355
13.76%	564.08	0.474
5.69%	230.77	0.546
7.05%	184.13	0.435
11.05%	218.18	0.216
3.93%	32.17	0.487

Let's head back to the dashboard now. In column E, we use a

VLOOKUP function to retrieve the possessions per minute data for each player in the lineup of both teams. Next, we multiply the possessions per minute from column E with the expected player minutes in column D to produce expected possessions in column F. This is the number of total possession a player is expected to get in this particular game, given their minutes.

STEP 2: CALCULATE TEAM POSSESSIONS

The next part of the process is to calculate team possessions by summing all the player possession values in column F by team. However, we need to apply an additional adjustment here: teams usually have very close to the same number of possessions in a game, so we must arrive at a a reasonable estimate that equalizes the possessions of both teams so that they are balanced. We can accomplish this in cells F13 and F27 using the following formula:

=AVERAGE(SUM(F2:F6,F8:F12),SUM(F16:F20,F22:F26))

Possessions/Min	Expected Possessions	On Court % ADJ	BPM/Min
0.361	7.687	46.74	-0.05
0.367	9.939	59.44	-0.01
0.467	11.105	52.22	-0.04
0.390	7.015	39.51	0.01
0.262	3.181	26.68	-0.03
	=AVERAGE(SUM(F2:F6,F8:F12),SUM(F16:F20,F22:F26))		
Possessions/Min	Expected Possessions	On Court % ADJ	BPM/Min
0.823	29.453	78.54	0.08
0.425	11.817	61.05	-0.03
0.419	10.986	57.62	-0.11

This equalizes both teams' estimated possessions at 105.36 in this example. Without this step, simply summing each team's possessions would leave us with 97.11 for Detroit and 113.59 for Atlanta (which would make little sense).

STEP 3: WEIGHT PLAYER-INFLUENCED POSSESSIONS

Now that we have player and team possessions estimated, we next need to determine how many team possessions a given player will be on the floor for ("On Court ADJ %" in column G). This is an important step because we need a way to strip the "per 100 possessions" component from BPM in order to reduce it to a per minute statistic.

Why is this an issue? Let's look at a quick example with Andre Drummond. Drummond has a BPM per 100 possessions of 3.00. In our game forecast, he is expected to use 14.856 possessions. If we try to divide his BPM by his expected individual possessions, we would get ((14.856/100)*3) = 0.45 BPM per minute. When you multiply that by his expected 36.13 minutes, you arrive at a spread value for Drummond of 16.10.

So either Andre Drummond is the greatest basketball player in the history of time or we've failed to account for something.

My money is on the second possibility. What we really want to know is how many of Detroit's anticipated 105.36 possessions Drummond is expected to be on the floor for and then *use that* as our adjustment factor for his BPM.

16.86	0.379	6.385	37.01
36.13	0.411	14.856	=(D6/48)*$F$13
ADJ MIN	Possessions/Min	Expected Possessions	On Court % ADJ
21.29	0.361	7.687	46.74
27.08	0.367	9.939	59.44
23.79	0.467	11.105	52.22
18.00	0.390	7.015	39.51
12.16	0.262	3.181	26.68
240.00		105.36	

We achieve this by dividing Andre's estimated minutes from cell D6 by 48 and then multiplying the result by Detroit's 105.36 estimated possessions. This gives us a value of 79.31 which is the number of Detroit possessions we expect Drummond to be on the court for. We perform this step for all players and then we're ready to complete our BPM transformation.

STEP 4: TRANSFORM BPM TO A PER MINUTE RATE

Column H is where we calculate each player's BPM per minute rate. This column uses another VLOOKUP function to retrieve the BPM value for a player and then weights the player's court presence for possessions, divides away a 1.2 multiplying factor added to the variable by Basketball-Reference.com and finally divides by expected player minutes.[3] Here's what it looks like for Andre Drummond:

= ((((Drummond BPM)*(On Court ADJ%/100))/1.2)/Minutes)

F	G	H	I
Expected Possessions	On Court % ADJ	BPM/Min	Spread Value
9.891	64.75	-0.01	-0.270
19.483	59.64	0.01	0.199
7.575	61.48	-0.02	-0.564
6.385	37.01	-0.10	-1.666
14.856	79.31	0.05	1.983
Expected Possessions	On Court % ADJ	BPM/Min	Spread Value
7.687	46.74	-0.05	-0.974
9.939	59.44	-0.01	-0.248
11.105	52.22	-0.04	-0.957
7.015	39.51	0.01	0.099
3.181	26.68	-0.03	-0.311
105.36		-0.18	-2.71

This results in a per minute BPM value of 0.05 in column H, and once multiplied with Drummond's expected minutes produces a total spread value of 1.983 in column I. From this we can estimate that with the given expected minutes, in this lineup and against Atlanta, Drummond is worth approximately 1.983 points to the spread differential. We then complete this process for all players to get their spread values and finish by summing the values by team (in cell I13 for Detroit and cell I27 for Atlanta). Detroit's lineup shows a game BPM of -2.71 and Atlanta is showing a value of -7.23. These negative numbers show that both teams are relatively weak, with Atlanta being the weaker team of the two.

GAME PREDICTIONS

With our team estimated BPM spread values in hand, we can finally make a game prediction between Detroit and Atlanta in columns M through Q. We import the team BPM spread values from I13 and I27 to M2 and M3. From here we convert the spread values to season long win percentages, transform the probabilities and then stabilize them so that they add up to 100% in a head-to-head matchup just like we did with our previous win shares model. Home court advantage is added along with the calculation in cells P2 and P3.

L	M	N	O	P	Q
Team	Raw Spread Value	Expected Season Win %	Transform %	Game Win %	Estimated Spread
Detroit Pistons	-2.71	41.08%	30.32%	57.12%	-2.16
Atlanta Hawks	-7.23	26.20%	15.44%	42.88%	2.16

Our final game spread estimate and moneyline fair odds are found in columns Q and R respectively. It appears that our BPM model is slightly more bullish on Detroit than our win shares model, with an estimated spread of -2.16 in their favour.

FINAL THOUGHTS

It's important to know that box score metrics like BPM become at least temporarily unreliable when players experience a change in their playing environment. For example, Andre Drummond is unlikely to maintain the same BPM after being traded to the Cleveland Cavaliers that he had with Detroit, due in part to the fact that some portion of his credited BPM was produced by playing in the Pistons' team environment. As a result, it's a good idea to take BPM values with a grain of salt when a player gets traded to a new team, or sees significant changes to his usage.

For those readers interested in modelling college basketball, I'd also point out that BPM values are available for NCAAB players on Sports-Reference.com if you click on each individual school.[4]

---

1. https://fansided.com/2019/01/08/nylon-calculus-best-advanced-stat/
2. https://www.basketball-reference.com/about/bpm.html
3. It's not actually necessary to divide by player minutes here only to multiply with them in the adjacent column. I just think it makes the spreadsheet easier to read as we can see both BPM per minute values and total spread contribution values.
4. https://www.sports-reference.com/cbb/schools/duke/2020.html

6

NHL EXPECTED GOALS MODEL

In this chapter, I'd like to show you a regression based player model for estimating expected goals per minute [GPM] in the NHL. It's similar in concept to the player models we've already looked at, but a few differences should be mentioned.

Firstly, as you're likely aware, NHL games contain 3 periods of play at 20 minutes each. This means that when we make player minute adjustments, all the expected minutes for each team should be scaled so that they add up to 300 minutes (5 skater positions * 60 minutes game duration).

Secondly, we'll obviously need a hockey-specific input variable or two - so we're going to use individual expected goals per 60 minutes (ixG/60) from NaturalStatTrick.com to forecast individual player goals per minute. We can then multiply these rates by expected player minutes and sum the totals by team to arrive at a game forecast.

Let's open the "NHL GPM" Excel file from the download package to get started. For this example, we'll be using the February 20th, 2020 game between the Montreal Canadiens and the Washington Captials.

Taking a cursory look at the main dashboard, much of the general structure should be starting to look familiar at this point. We enter the player names in column A for the away team and column L for the home team. The next 4 columns automatically retrieve team and position information as well as calculating % of minutes and adjusting total team minutes so that they fit into our 300 minute constraint.

A	B	C	D	E
			101.61%	300.00
AWAY FORWARDS	TEAM	POSITION	MIN %	ADJ MIN
Tomas Tatar	MTL	L	5.47%	16.16
Phillip Danault	MTL	C, L	6.26%	18.49
Brendan Gallagher	MTL	R	5.64%	16.66
Jonathan Drouin	MTL	L	5.27%	15.57
Nick Suzuki	MTL	C	5.31%	15.67
Joel Armia	MTL	R	5.77%	17.03
Paul Byron	MTL	L	4.60%	13.59
Max Domi	MTL	C	5.71%	16.85
Ilya Kovalchuk	L.A, MTL	L	5.80%	17.13
Jordan Weal	MTL	C	4.46%	13.16
Nate Thompson	MTL	C	4.26%	12.57
Nick Cousins	MTL	C	4.49%	13.25
AWAY DEFENSE	TEAM	POSITION	MIN %	ADJ MIN
Ben Chiarot	MTL	D	7.81%	23.07
Shea Weber	MTL	D	8.09%	23.87

Columns F and Q contain the new ixG/60 input variable from NaturalStatTrick.com. Let's go over how that was decided upon as an input variable before moving on. If you open the "GPM Regression" sheet inside the file, you'll see that we conducted some tests to determine how useful ixG/60 might be for predicting player goals per minute using the 3 part process from chapter 3. While NaturalStatTrick.com has a number of interesting player rate statistics like Corsi, Fenwick and high danger scoring chances (HDCF), ixG/60 is a simple introduction to this type of player modelling and serves as a good example.[1]

A	B	C	D	E	F	G	H	I
In-Sample	Split Half	Out-Sample			In-Sample	Split Half	Out-Sample	
85.06%	87.98%	74.69%			85.06%	87.98%	74.69%	
ixG/60 2018	ixG/60 2017	ixG/60 2017	2018 GPM		ixG/60 2018	ixG/60 2017	ixG/60 2017	2018 GPM
0.77	0.94	0.94	0.025		0.013	0.016	0.016	0.025
0.36	0.41	0.41	0.004		0.006	0.007	0.007	0.004
0.96	0.95	0.95	0.023		0.016	0.016	0.016	0.023
0.7	0.72	0.72	0.015		0.012	0.012	0.012	0.015
0.91	0.82	0.82	0.015		0.015	0.014	0.014	0.015
1.25	1.1	1.1	0.027		0.021	0.018	0.018	0.027
0.61	0.75	0.75	0.012		0.010	0.013	0.013	0.012
0.38	0.31	0.31	0.009		0.006	0.005	0.005	0.009
0.34	0.23	0.23	0.008		0.006	0.004	0.004	0.008
0.54	0.56	0.56	0.011		0.009	0.009	0.009	0.011

GOALS PER MINUTE REGRESSION

We first go to NaturalStatTrick.com and download player rate data from the 2017-2018 and 2018-2019 seasons and filter for players that have played over 400 minutes in a season. We then isolate a few variables using in-sample correlation indicators and narrow our search down to ixG/60 in this example. While Corsi, Fenwick, Shots/60 and High Danger Scoring Chances were considered, we'll keep this model simple to aid understanding. Readers are encouraged to conduct their own experiments using multiple input variables that show promise.

Using the basic testing process from chapter 3, ixG/60 either as a per 60 minutes stat (columns A to D) or reduced to a per minute stat (columns F to I) appears to show encouraging results for us. This is hardly surprising considering the underlying information contained in an xG statistic, but it's reassuring to see that our "predictive power" test confirms that this is an input variable worth exploring.[2] After concluding the tests we run a regression using player goals per minute as the Y variable and ixG/60 (as the per minute rate) as the X variable which produces the following result:

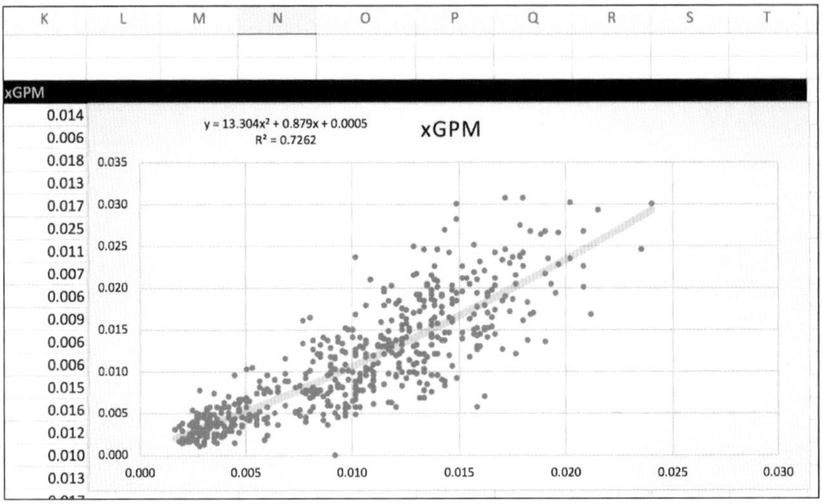

Noticing a slight curvature in the scatterplot, a polynomial[3] regression equation was used instead of a standard linear equation. The equation produced here is as follows:

Player GPM = (0.0005)+(0.879*ixG) + (13.304 * (ixG^2))

You can see that there is a fair bit of dispersion from the regression line. This could be due to the inherent randomness of hockey goal scoring performance, or an indication that we might want to consider a more strongly indicative input variable. That being said, our residuals appear to be consistent with random error[4] (no problematic patterns detected) and our graph shows a decent positive relationship.[5] Having created a regression equation which we think is reasonably predictive, we can head back to the main dashboard sheet and calculate GPM values for each player.

ESTIMATING PLAYER GOALS PER MINUTE

Back in the main dashboard sheet in columns F and Q, our model retrieves player ixG/60 values from the "Skaters 2019-2020" database sheet using Excel's VLOOKUP function. In columns G and R we then apply our regression equation to the ixG/60 values, remembering to reduce them to a per minute rate. After completing this, we multiply each player's expected goals per minute rate by their expected ice time to produce expected goals for the game in question. This has been completed in columns H and S.

E	F	G	H
300.00			3.15
ADJ MIN	IXG/60	xGPM	xGOALS
16.16	0.81	0.015	0.239
18.49	0.59	0.010	=G4*E4
16.66	1.5	0.031	0.513
15.57	0.66	0.012	0.183

Finally, we sum the expected goals for each team in cells H1 and S1. Here we see that Montreal has a base xG expectation of 3.15 goals and Washington has a base xG expectation of 3.37. We will however have to adjust for starting goalies, so let's do that now.

STARTING GOALIES

No hockey forecast is complete without considering starting goalies, so let's add that to our calculations. When we're done we'll add a few finishing touches to the model and be ready to make a game prediction.

In row 23 you'll see that we have entered the names of the starting goalies for both teams. For this model I wanted to keep things relatively simple, so our goalie adjustment is going to be xG against divided by league average to produce a percentage adjustment. If you go to the "Goalies 2019-2020" database sheet you'll see that the league average xG against is around 2.56 (cell AH2). Back in the dashboard sheet, we retrieve each starting goalie's xG against and divide by the league average. This produces the "ADJ%" number that we then use to adjust opponent expected goals. Pictured below is Carey Price's adjustment number, which is calculated to be 0.933. This means that Washington can be expected to score around 93.3% of their base expected goal total from cell S1.

20	Xavier Ouellet	MTL	D	4.27%	12.61
21	Christian Folin	MTL	D	4.95%	14.61
22	AWAY GOALIE	TEAM	POSITION	xGA	ADJ%
23	Carey Price	MTL	G	2.39	0.933
24					

From here, we multiply each team's base expected goals by their opponent's goalie adjustment % number to create a game expected goals value. You can see these values in cells H/I23 and S/T23. We finish the calculations off by adding a 0.28 goal differential advantage for the home team and then we're ready to make a forecast. Montreal is expected to produce 2.996 goals while Washington is expected to produce 3.285 goals.

GAME PREDICTION

The game prediction function is located in rows 26, 27 and 28 of the main dashboard. You'll see that the first two columns (B & C) have imported the two team names and their xG values (2.996 & 3.285). The next two columns simply calculate the expected goal differential between the two teams and the expected combined goal total.

Then we get to the forecasted probabilities in cells F27 and F28.

You may be wondering why there isn't a competing poisson matrix to calculate probabilities here (like we used in SSME1), and the answer is that *we don't actually need one*. While you certainly could calculate the probabilities with a poisson matrix, I wanted to show you another way using expected goal differential.

Every goal differential implies a long-term win probability. Using a logistic formula I found at Mike Beuoy's Inpredictable.com website[6], we can take the expected 0.29 goal differential between Washington and Montreal and calculate how often either team should win. Here's the formula:

=1/(1+EXP((-(HIA+HOME-AWAY)/1.318)))

Where HIA is home ice advantage, and HOME and AWAY are the expected goals above an average team for both home and away. League average NHL teams are scoring around 3.03 goals this year so Washington's goals above average number (with HIA already included) is 0.255 which can be found on the sheet in cell S/T24. Montreal's corresponding value is -0.034 in cell H/I24. Since the 0.28 home advantage has already been factored in, this leaves us with the following equation in cell F28:

=1/(1+EXP((-(0.255–(0.034))/1.318)))

= **55.46%**

Washington's win probability is 55.46%, leaving Montreal with a 44.54% win probability for this game.

FINAL THOUGHTS

Pinnacle sports had this game priced at 1.54 for Washington and 2.66 for Montreal. That diverges from our estimate (1.80/2.25) by a substantial amount, and for that reason we may have to consider whether we're missing something here. For what it's worth Montreal (our model's value pick) did end up winning the game 4-3 in overtime and our forecast was in line with MoneyPuck.com's probability estimates for this game (54.04% for Washington). We'd ideally want to track and test many more games to know how good this model really is, but it's certainly an improvement over a team-level model.

Finally, I've included a few extras bits of information in this model for you to experiment with - you'll see estimated shots for each player in columns I and T, team shots in cells M27 and M28, and goalie expected saves in cells N27 and N28. These are just a few odds and ends for you to see the possibility of extending a model like this into player prop bets. See what you can find. Happy hunting.

---

1. You may wish to experiment with adding more input variables from NaturalStatTrick.com to your model attempts. When you go to the site, select "Players", then "Individuals" and then "Rates" as opposed to count statistics. Lots of possibilities for input variables exist.
2. If you're interested in learning more about what goes into an xG stat itself, take a look at MoneyPuck.com/about.htm. Lots of great information about creating an expected goals statistic is freely available online and well worth Googling to learn more about.
3. https://en.wikipedia.org/wiki/Polynomial_regression
4. https://blog.minitab.com/blog/adventures-in-statistics-2/why-you-need-to-check-your-residual-plots-for-regression-analysis
5. When looking at residuals, we want to see an absence of pattern which suggests random error. If there is a pattern or shape to a regression's residuals it implies that there is a systematic error at play and that we've missed something important.
6. https://www.inpredictable.com/2018/10/betting-market-rankings-for-nhl.html

7

MLB WRC+ MODEL

In this chapter I'd like to walk you through a player based MLB model for estimating runs scored in the first inning [RIFI]. While full game probabilities for baseball are tricky to get right with an Excel model, smaller markets like RIFI props can show glimpses of positive expected value.

Let's open up the "MLB WRC" Excel file and get started.

You'll see that we first have to enter the number of anticipated Houston Astros trash can banging signals in cell K23.

I'm kidding.

Before we get started for real, let's go over a simple way to estimate runs scored in the first inning of a ballgame that comes from Michael Shackleford's exceedingly helpful website WizardofOdds.com. Once we've done that we'll walk through the player based model presented here and compare the two forecasts to see if we've made a reasonable estimation.

MICHAEL SHACKLEFORD REGRESSION FOR RIFI

Over at WizardofOdds.com, Michael Shackleford used multiple years of MLB data to create a simple regression equation for runs scored in the first inning.[1] Two methods were presented, but we'll use the simpler of the two here. It is as follows:

Probability of RIFI = 0.2554 + 0.0304 * (Game Total)

So if the game total is 8.5 runs (as it was when Houston played Pittsburgh on June 25th, 2019 which will be our example game), the probability of a run in the first inning is:

Probability of RIFI = 0.2554 + 0.0304 * (8.5)

= **51.38%**

Taking this as our baseline estimate for this game, let's turn our attention now to the "MLB WRC" Excel file and see if we can do a bit better using player lineup information.

RIFI EXCEL MODEL

Opening up the main dashboard sheet, you'll once again see that the structure is similar to models we've looked at already. Player lineups for each team are inputted into columns A and K and the model retrieves various player stats from the "database" sheets using Excel's VLOOKUP function. All of the data comes from FanGraphs.com. The model inputs we'll be using are weighted runs created plus (WRC+)[2] and Field Independent Pitching (FIP)[3], along with some adjustments for platoon effects and expected plate appearances. If you'd like to know more about these statistics, I'd recommend taking a look at the very helpful library of baseball stats at FanGraphs.com (check the end notes for a few links).

A	B	C	D	E	F
TEAM SUM		927	937	814	3.6
AWAY BATTERS	Team	Proj wRC+	wRC+ v L	wRC+ v R	Est PA
Kevin Newman	Pirates	83	144	5	1
Corey Dickerson	Pirates	109	100	120	1
Starling Marte	Pirates	111	95	119	1
Josh Bell	Pirates	120	101	116	0.6
Melky Cabrera	Pirates	104	127	93	0
Colin Moran	Pirates	101	42	113	0
Jose Osuna	Pirates	102	119	19	0
Elias Diaz	Pirates	95	151	98	0
Adam Frazier	Pirates	102	58	131	0
AWAY STARTING PITCHER	Team	Hand	Proj FIP	FIP v AVG	Est RA/IP
Trevor Williams	Pirates	R	4.53	0.833	0.503

After entering the batter lineup information, the next 3 columns for each player are overall WRC+ and WRC+ when facing either left or right handed pitchers. WRC+ is handy because it's standardized so that a rating of 100 is average, which means we can easily create a player weighted adjustment for team performance by combining WRC+ and expected plate appearances. If a player has a WRC+ against left handed pitchers of 111, we can take that to mean he will be expected to hit around 11% better than an average player in this situation. We can then multiply this by expected plate appearances to estimate a given player's contribution to run creation in the first inning.

C	D	E	F	G
927	937	814	3.6	0.15
Proj wRC+	wRC+ v L	wRC+ v R	Est PA	Base wRC+
83	144	5	1	-0.170
109	100	120	1	0.090
111	95	119	1	=((C5/100)-1)*F5
120	101	116	0.6	0.120
104	127	93	0	0.000
101	42	113	0	0.000

Plate appearances for baseball are the player "opportunity unit" in the same sense that minutes are for basketball and hockey. Because we are only interested in first inning performance, plate appearances are manually estimated for each team's starting lineup by taking total batters faced per inning by opponent and distributing it from the top of the lineup down in columns F and P.[4] You'll see that in this game example we're expecting Trevor Williams to face 4.43 batters in the first inning so Houston's expected plate appearances are distributed accordingly. Gerrit Cole is expected to face 3.6 batters, so we adjust the Pittsburgh batting opportunities in the same way.

A	B	C	D	E	F
TEAM SUM		927	937	814	3.6
AWAY BATTERS	Team	Proj wRC+	wRC+ v L	wRC+ v R	Est PA
Kevin Newman	Pirates	83	144	5	1
Corey Dickerson	Pirates	109	100	120	1
Starling Marte	Pirates	111	95	119	1
Josh Bell	Pirates	120	101	116	0.6

ESTIMATING 1ST INNING BATTING STRENGTH

We now have WRC+ above average weighted by expected plate appearances for both teams in cells H1 & I1 for Pittsburgh and R1 & S1 for Houston. The pitching hand of the opposing pitcher ("R" or "L" in cells C13 and M13) determines which WRC+ above average calculation the model uses. Pitching handedness is entered into the sheet manually. We then add the WRC+ above average adjustment to a value of 100 to produce a performance expectation for both teams in cells I13 and S13. Pittsburgh has an expected batting performance value of 0.995 and Houston's value is 1.015. This naturally tells us that Houston should bat slightly better than Pittsburgh. Now let's take a look at pitching.

H	I	J	K	L	M
0.40	-0.464		TEAM SUM		1012
wRC+ L	wRC+ R		HOME BATTERS	Team	Proj wRC+
0.440	-0.950		George Springer	Astros	127
0.000	0.200		Jose Altuve	Astros	130
-0.050	0.190		Alex Bregman	Astros	140
0.006	0.096		Michael Brantley	Astros	119
0.000	0.000		Yordan Alvarez	Astros	99
0.000	0.000		Myles Straw	Astros	89
0.000	0.000		Yuli Gurriel	Astros	109
0.000	0.000		Josh Reddick	Astros	109
0.000	0.000		Robinson Chirinos	Astros	90
Est RA/5	Est WRC%		HOME STARTING PITCHER	Team	Hand
=IF(M13="R",100+I1,100+H1)/100				Astros	R

PITCHER FIP & EXPECTED RUNS AGAINST

The model retrieves FIP values for both pitchers in row 13. We then perform some very basic calculations to get a rough estimate of expected runs against per inning by dividing pitcher FIP by 9 and then multiplying it by the opposing team's WRC+ batting adjustment value. The final 1st inning runs against expectations are found in cell G13 for Pittsburgh and cell Q13 for Houston.

Est RA/IP	Est RA/FI
0.503	0.511

ESTIMATING PROBABILITIES

Run scoring has been modelled reasonably well by others using the negative binomial and/or enby distribution and that's precisely what we'll be using here in rows 18, 19 and 20 of the main dashboard sheet.[5]

Negative Binomial Calcs	Expected Runs	B Parameter	R Parameter	Probability of 0 Runs
Pirates	0.511	0.499	1.024	66.08%
Astros	0.369	0.480	0.770	73.95%

Of course, we don't need the entire distribution estimate in this case - we only need to know the probability that neither team scores a run in order to infer the probability that either team scores one or more. This saves us a bit of work.

Here's how we do it using a process outlined on the website "Walk Like A Sabermetrician"[6]:

Step 1: Estimate negative binomial parameters "B" and "R using the following formulas:

B Parameter = (0.1345 * Runs Against) + 0.43

R Parameter = Runs Against/(0.1345 * Runs Against + 0.43)

Pittsburgh: B = 0.499, R = 1.024

Houston: B = 0.480, R = 0.770

Step 2: Calculate the probability of each team giving up zero runs with the following formula:

Probability of 0 runs = ((1 + B)^(-R))

Pittsburgh: 66.08%

Houston: 73.95%

Step 3: Calculate the probability of neither team giving up a run

---

= 66.08% * 73.95% = 48.87%

RIFI = 1-48.87%

RIFI = 51.13%

You'll see that the final probability outputs are found on the main dashboard sheet in cells G19 and G20.

	TEAM	SP	EXP RA	Expected Runs Total	RIFI?	PROB %	FAIR ODDS
AWAY	Pirates	Trevor Williams	0.511	0.880	YES	51.13%	1.96
HOME	Astros	Gerrit Cole	0.369		NO	48.87%	2.05

FINAL THOUGHTS

Ultimately no runs were scored in the first inning of this game. It's interesting to note though that our player based model estimated the probability of a run in the first inning for this game at 51.13%, which wasn't significantly different from the probability estimate given by Michael Shackleford's regression equation (51.38%).

We could almost certainly improve our forecast by making tweaks to the expected pitcher FIP, the number of expected batters faced and other input variables. Still, we're not too far off the mark on this relatively simple prop bet. I would encourage readers to experiment with making their own adjustments to this and other models in the book. It's the best way to learn and develop your own unique approach.

---

1. https://wizardofodds.com/games/sports-betting/mlb/old-stuff/
2. https://library.fangraphs.com/offense/wrc/
3. https://library.fangraphs.com/pitching/fip/
4. You could add this calculation to the sheet, but it's easy enough to simply look up the total batters faces per inning by team on FanGraphs.com.
5. http://walksaber.blogspot.com/2012/07/on-run-distributions-pt-6.html
6. http://walksaber.blogspot.com/2012/07/on-run-distributions-pt-6.html

8

MODEL DOWNLOAD PACKAGE

Just like the first volume of *Statistical Sports Models in Excel*, I've included working copies of all of the models and techniques I'll be discussing in this book as a downloadable collection of Excel spreadsheets. This way, you'll be able to follow along with what we cover. Although I'm biased, I think the utility of this download file is worth many times the cost of this book, and I hope once you go through it you'll feel the same way. Click the following link to download the entire model package file from MediaFire:

SSME Spreadsheet Models Download

For readers of the print edition, here is the download link:

http://www.mediafire.com/file/etf7q6jvxxnvykm/SSME2.zip/file

Please note that MediaFire is occasionally finicky and some readers have experienced technical issues successfully accessing the download package in the past. If that happens to you while trying to enter the link into your web browser, try removing the "**/file**" from the end of the URL. This fix has helped most readers to successfully access the download package. Should you try both ways and still encounter issues, please contact me on Twitter **@Gingfacekillah** and I'll help you get the download sorted.

I'd very much appreciate it if you kept the location of this download link to yourself, although I recognize it's only a matter of time before it become ubiquitous on the internet. Feel free to use these models for your own purposes, explore new ideas, or try tweaking them for different sports. If you come up with anything interesting I'd love to hear about it. If you make reference to them, I would kindly request a link back to my twitter page.

Finally, I'd recommend making a copy of the original models so that you have working copies and originals. This way, if anything goes wrong while you're experimenting on your own, you have the original models to revert back to. Once you've downloaded the file and made yourself a backup copy we're ready to move on.

DERIVATIVES

9

UNDERSTANDING DERIVATIVE RELATIONSHIPS

The term 'derivative' comes from financial markets, where it refers to a financial instrument that derives its value mainly from the price of another financial instrument. In sports betting, derivative markets work in a very similar way. For example, first half totals can be created (or derived) from the value of a full game total line. Almost every main betting market line implies a handful of derivatives that are closely related to it. This means at least two things:

1. It's possible to calculate a fair derivative price from a main betting market line; and

2. If there is sufficient deviation in the derivative relationship there may be betting value.

Many sharp books move their derivative market prices in synch with their main market moves, meaning there isn't much value in betting them without additional modelling insight. However, some books are slow to adjust the prices on their derivative lines when their main markets have moved. When this happens, it's possible to find betting value on the derivative market in question.

As I mentioned in the "Benter Boost" chapter of SSME1, there is an inherent advantage in acknowledging that you are up against superior competition and adjusting your strategy accordingly. Reverse engineering markets through derivative relationships capitalizes on this by using the aggregate accuracy of highly liquid markets to identify possible opportunities in smaller ones.

To put it succinctly, if a market appears too sharp to beat with our currently available methods, it's sometimes possible to use that strength to beat smaller, lower limit markets that are closely related. This usually works well as long as you keep in mind the direction of the implications. That is to say, we don't want to use prop betting lines to infer that a pointspread market is inefficient - we are looking to use large markets to inform our opinions on smaller ones exclusively.

PROP DERIVATIVES

This same simple understanding of derivatives can also be used to help assess prop betting lines. If a game total combined with a spread or moneyline implies a team total, then a corresponding player prop implies a certain proportional level of player contribution.

For example, if the Toronto Raptors have a team total of 111.5 and Fred VanVleet has a points prop line of 19.5 points, there is an implication that his proportional contribution to the Raptors' scoring production will be 17.49%. A quick investigation into VanVleet's season numbers shows that his median percentage contribution to the Raptors' point production is 15.57%. This example ends up being a small difference, but it's a different way of potentially uncovering a discrepancy we might want to explore.

Finding inconsistencies in the trickle-down "chain of derivatives" can open up potential opportunities for those paying attention to them. With that in mind, let's take a look at a few example models. As for the prop derivatives idea specifically, I'll leave that for readers to investigate further on their own.

10

NHL TEAM TOTAL DERIVATIVE MODEL

In this chapter I'd like to walk you through a method to estimate team totals in the NHL. Team totals, like many betting lines, can be derived or reverse engineered from larger market lines. This makes them an approachable place to start if you're somewhat new to modelling.

Let's give it a shot together. Open the "NHL Team Totals" Excel file from the download package to follow along.

In sports like the NBA or NFL it's easy to figure out an implied team total because betting lines exist for both the total and the pointspread. With a little simple math, each team's forecasted point production is easily calculated. It's a little bit trickier in moneyline sports like the NHL or MLB though because we first need to determine the implied goal or run differential. The first task necessary to accomplish this is to calculate the implied total goals or runs for the game.

STEP 1: REVERSE ENGINEER THE IMPLIED TOTAL GOALS

Every NHL game total line (including the O/U prices) implies an expected integer number of total goals. Our first step is to calculate this. This can be accomplished by reverse engineering the problem using Excel's Solver. What we want to do is use Solver to calculate the exact number of total goals that would be required to produce the current goal total line, remembering to account for the bookmaker's commission.

Let's get on it. In this example from February 22nd, 2020, the Colorado Avalanche were playing the Los Angeles Kings. Our first step is to input the game total and prices into cells A2/3 and B2/3. You'll see this has already been completed here - the game total line is 5.5 and the over/under prices are 1.892 and 2.000 respectively. The sheet then automatically calculates the no-vig or commission-free probabilities in cells D2 and D3. A simple method for vig removal is used that divides each implied probability by the total probability of both prices:

A	B	C	D	E	F	G
TOTAL	TOTAL PRICE	VIG PROB %	NO-VIG PROB %			xGOALS
5.5	1.892	52.85%	51.39%	Over %	51.39%	5.75
5.5	2.000	50.00%	48.61%	Poisson %	51.39%	
		102.85%				
				Over %	D2	
				Poisson %	1-POISSON(A3,G2,TRUE)	

Over Price: [1/1.892] = 52.85%

Under Price: [1/2.00] = 50.00%

Total Probability: [52.85% + 50.00%] = 102.85%

Over No-Vig: [52.85%/102.85%] = 51.39%

Under No-Vig: [50.00%/102.85%] = 48.61%

Now that both of our no-vig prices add up to 100%, we can use Solver to reverse engineer the exact number of expected goals that would produce this line. To do that, we instruct Solver to adjust a cell with our estimated total goals (cell G2) until the Poisson probability of being over the betting market total line number equals the implied probability of the no-vig over line. When these two probabilities match on the sheet (cells F2 and F3), we have found our true implied total goals for the game.

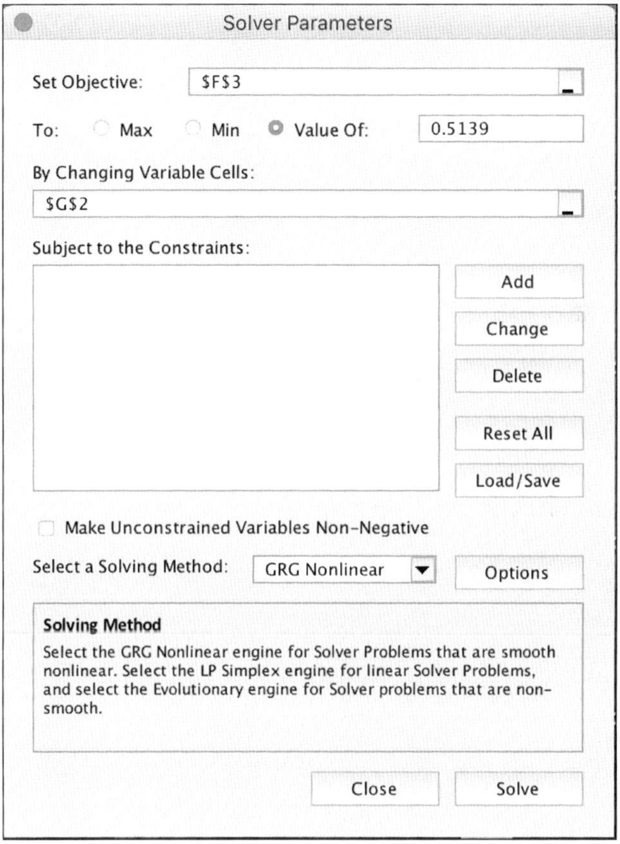

We open Solver and make the objective cell F3, "to a value of" 0.5139 (which is the probability we are trying to match in cell F2), by changing cell G2. Set "GRG Nonlinear" as the solving method and click "Solve". When Solver arrives at an answer, our true implied goal total for this game can be found in cell G2. In this case 5.75 goals is the expected true total for this game.

STEP 2: REVERSE ENGINEER GOAL DIFFERENTIAL

Now that we have the estimated total goals, we need to estimate the implied goal differential between the two teams from the moneyline. Every moneyline, when combined with a total, implies a strength differential that can be quantified into goal differential.

First we input the moneyline prices for both teams and convert them to no-vig probabilities using the same process we used before. Here we have Colorado at 1.666 in cell B9 and Los Angeles at 2.350 in cell B10. The no-vig probabilities are calculated and outputted into cells D9 and D10.

8	TEAM	ODDS	VIG PROB %	NO-VIG PROB %
9	COL	1.666	60.02%	58.52%
10	LAK	2.350	42.55%	41.48%
11			102.58%	

Then we take the natural logarithm [LN] of each probability from cells D9 and D10 in and output them into cells E9 and E10.

TEAM	ODDS	VIG PROB %	NO-VIG PROB %	LN
COL	1.666	60.02%	58.52%	=LN(D9)
LAK	2.350	42.55%	41.48%	-0.88
		102.58%		

Next, using regression values taken from the website Inpredictable.com[1], we multiply the logarithm values by -1.318 and calculate the absolute difference between the two teams using the ABS function in Excel.

LN*-1.318	ABS Goal Diff
0.71	0.45
1.16	0.45

This gives us an estimated absolute goal differential of 0.45. We can now take this goal differential and combine it with the implied total goals to calculate an expected team total.

STEP 3: CALCULATE IMPLIED TEAM TOTAL

Calculating the expected team totals with our freshly acquired data is easy. We simply instruct Excel to add half the goal differential to half the expected total for the favourite and subtract half the goal differential from half the expected total for the underdog using the following formula:

NO-VIG PROB %	LN	LN*-1.318	ABS Goal Diff	Implied Total	Team Totals
58.52%	-0.54	0.71	0.45	5.75	3.10
41.48%	-0.88	1.16	=IF(D10>D9,(0.5*H9)+(0.5*G10),(0.5*H9)-(0.5*G10))		

Doing this for both teams produces the expected team totals in cells I9 and I10 of the sheet. Colorado is expected to score 3.10 goals, while Los Angeles is expected to score 2.65.

STEP 4: COMPARE TO MARKET PRICES

We're finally to take these numbers and compare them to market prices in our search for betting value. Checking the market, we see that the following prices were available minutes before puck drop:

Colorado O/U 3.5 goals | 2.19/1.735

Los Angeles O/U 2.5 goals | 2.00/1.877

We go to cells B13 and B14 and enter the team total lines. Then in cells E/F13 & E/F14 we enter the decimal prices for the over and under of each team total.

11			102.58%					
12	TEAM	TEAM TOTAL LINE	OVER %	UNDER %	OVER PRICE	UNDER PRICE	EV OVER	EV UNDER
13	COL	3.5	37.59%	62.41%	2.190	1.735	-17.68%	8.28%
14	LAK	2.5	49.40%	50.60%	2.000	1.877	-1.20%	-5.03%
15								
16								

Colorado under 3.5 goals looks surprisingly good at 8.28%, which would be our model's value play in this situation. As it turns out, the Avalanche beat the Kings 2-1 in overtime, which would have cashed our hypothetical under 3.5 goals bet at 1.735 nicely.

1. https://www.inpredictable.com/2018/10/betting-market-rankings-for-nhl.html

11

EPL EXACT SCORES

Normally when we build a sports betting model, we are trying to produce a point estimate[1] so that we can apply the appropriate probability distribution and generate fair prices to compare with the market.

However, as we saw in the last chapter, we can also reverse that process and start with fair prices, run them "backwards" through the right probability distribution and arrive at a point estimate. This reverse engineered point estimate can then be used to inform our betting decisions on smaller markets.

Let's give that a go here with the English Premier League.

On February 22nd, 2020, Leicester played a match at home against Manchester City. The final score was 0-1 in favour of Manchester, and model I'm about to show you indicated that this was the most probable exact score outcome.

How did it do that?

It might have simply gotten lucky.

However, the conceptual answer I was angling towards was that it leveraged the strength of 1X2 market derivative relationships to reverse engineer a forecast, using the larger market to inform a smaller one.

Exact score markets are a great example of how understanding derivative relationships can assist your modelling efforts and the search for betting value, with relatively light effort.

Let me show you how it works. Open the "EPL Exact Scores" Excel file to follow along with this chapter.

DETERMINE LEAGUE AVERAGE GOALS

Our first step is to gather data from a reasonably large sample of games and observe how the data behaves. Specifically, we're looking to determine the mean goals scored for both home and away teams, the variance of goal scoring and the general distribution.

In the "Determine Average Goals" sheet, you can see that I've gathered game result data for the EPL from 2015 to 2020 from Joseph Buchdahl's football-data.co.uk website.[2] In cells F2 and G2 we find the average goals scored for both home and away. In cells H2 and I2 we find the variance of home and away goal scoring.

C	D	E	F	G	H	I
AWAY GOALS	HOME TEAM	HOME GOALS	AWAY GOALS AVG	HOME GOALS AVG	AWAY GOALS VAR	HOME GOALS VAR
1	Bournemouth	0	1.215	1.540	1.418	1.658
2	Chelsea	2				
2	Everton	2				
2	Leicester	4				
0	Man United	1				
3	Norwich	1				

Normally the poisson distribution would be the obvious choice for modelling soccer goals. In this case however, we notice something interesting - in a sample of over 1,700 games the variance of goal scoring appears to exceed the mean for both home and away teams. This suggests that using a poisson distribution for the EPL may not be the best choice, despite the fact it is a very common probability distribution to apply to soccer scoring. Generally, when the variance exceeds the mean for discrete count data like soccer goals, a distribution that accounts for this divergence is more appropriate. One obvious example is the negative binomial distribution. This is because unlike the poisson distribution, the negative binomial distribution allows us some flexibility when the variance of the data exceeds its mean (also known as being over dispersed). When using the poisson distribution, the variance and the mean of the data are supposed to be the same.

Let's move forward on the basis that, for now, a negative binomial distribution is what we'd like to try in this scenario.[3]

DETERMINE EXACT SCORE GOAL FREQUENCY

Our next step is to determine how often each possible exact score has occurred. In the "Find Goal Frequency" sheet, you'll see that this has been completed in columns L, M, N and O. We take the same data that we used in the previous sheet and count the number of occurrences for each exact score possibility using the COUNTIFS function in Excel in column N. We then divide the frequency of occurrence by the total number of games in the dataset to calculate the exact score frequency in column O.

K	L	M	N	O	P
		EXACT SCORE			
	HOME	AWAY	Freq	Percentage	
	0	0	123	7.01%	
	0	1	114	6.50%	
	=COUNTIFS($B$2:$B$1755,M5,$D$2:$D$1755,L5)				
	0	3	53	3.02%	
	0	4	23	1.31%	
	0	5	4	0.23%	
	0	6	2	0.11%	

You'll probably recall that we did something very similar to this in the first volume of Statistical Sports Models in Excel, but notice that this time we are using exact score rather than individual team scoring frequencies.

ZERO INFLATE THE NEGATIVE BINOMIAL DISTRIBUTION

After calculating the exact score frequencies, we want to adjust our probability distribution to allow it to better account for the fact that lower scoring games occur more frequently in the EPL than a generic negative binomial distribution might expect. To do this, we use the same process outlined in SSME1, where we compare the hypothetical frequencies of a competing negative binomial matrix using average home and away goals to the actual observed exact score frequencies and make a percentage adjustment for each relevant exact score possibility. The only difference this time around is that we're adjusting a negative binomial distribution matrix rather than a poisson.

A	B	C	D	E
Away Teams		K	PROB %	CUMUL %
MEAN	1.21	0	0.325372023	0.325372023
VARIANCE	1.42	1	0.338393936	0.663765959
		2	0.200284187	0.864050146
B	0.1678318	3	0.088622161	0.952672307
R	7.2368314	4	0.032594311	0.985266618
KURTOSIS	2.0898564	5	0.01052712	0.995793737
SKEW	1.8437232	6	0.003085469	0.998879207
		7	0.000838496	0.999717703
		8	0.000214446	0.999932149
		9	5.21752E-05	0.999984324
		10	1.21747E-05	0.999996499
		11	2.74169E-06	0.999999241
		12	5.98798E-07	0.999999839
		13	1.2734E-07	0.999999967
		14	2.64529E-08	0.999999993
		15	5.38227E-09	0.999999999

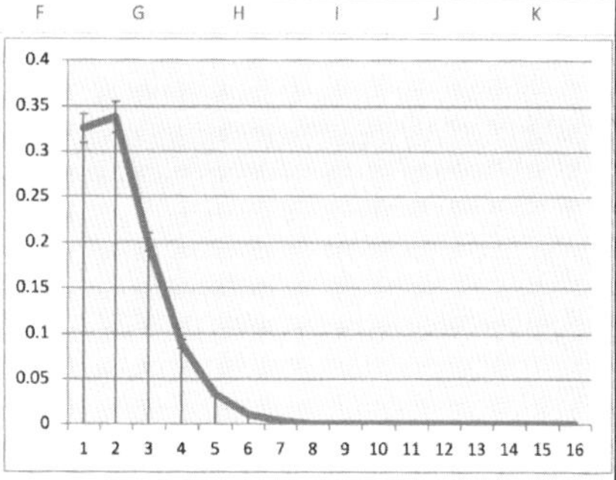

The "NegBinomial" sheet calculates the hypothetical goal scoring distributions for home and away teams using the league averages we calculated in the "Determine Average Goals" sheet (1.215 for away & 1.540 for home). It also calculates the individual team scoring distributions for our specific game matchup lower in the sheet.

In the "NegBinomial Calcs" sheet you'll see 3 matrices that function the same way as they did in SSME1[4]. The first matrix calculates the hypothetical frequency of exact scores using the negative binomial distribution probabilities from the top of the "NegBinomial" sheet. These are our base expectations given a home average of 1.54 goals and an away average of 1.21 goals.

A	B	C		D	E	F	G	H	I	J
Home Average	Away Average									
1.54	1.21			0	1	2	3	4	5	6
				0.325372	0.3383939	0.2002842	0.0886222	0.0325943	0.0105271	0.0030855
		0	0.2267033	7.38%	7.67%	4.54%	2.01%	0.74%	0.24%	0.07%
		1	0.3243636	10.55%	10.98%	6.50%	2.87%	1.06%	0.34%	0.10%
		2	0.2435613	7.92%	8.24%	4.88%	2.16%	0.79%	0.26%	0.08%
		3	0.1276889	4.15%	4.32%	2.56%	1.13%	0.42%	0.13%	0.04%
		4	0.0524727	1.71%	1.78%	1.05%	0.47%	0.17%	0.06%	0.02%
Hypothetical		5	0.0179957	0.59%	0.61%	0.36%	0.16%	0.06%	0.02%	0.01%
Expected		6	0.005356	0.17%	0.18%	0.11%	0.05%	0.02%	0.01%	0.00%
Frequencies		7	0.0014207	0.05%	0.05%	0.03%	0.01%	0.00%	0.00%	0.00%
		8	0.0003423	0.01%	0.01%	0.01%	0.00%	0.00%	0.00%	0.00%
		9	7.603E-05	0.00%	0.00%	0.00%	0.00%	0.00%	0.00%	0.00%
		10	1.574E-05	0.00%	0.00%	0.00%	0.00%	0.00%	0.00%	0.00%
		11	3.062E-06	0.00%	0.00%	0.00%	0.00%	0.00%	0.00%	0.00%
		12	5.644E-07	0.00%	0.00%	0.00%	0.00%	0.00%	0.00%	0.00%
		13	9.911E-08	0.00%	0.00%	0.00%	0.00%	0.00%	0.00%	0.00%
		14	1.666E-08	0.00%	0.00%	0.00%	0.00%	0.00%	0.00%	0.00%
		15	2.693E-09	0.00%	0.00%	0.00%	0.00%	0.00%	0.00%	0.00%

The second matrix shows the actual observed frequencies of exact scores from our EPL dataset in the "Find Goal Frequency" sheet. We can see that there is a significant difference between the hypothetical and actual frequencies - the actual observed frequencies are "inflated" towards lower scoring outcomes. Hopefully this should be sounding familiar to you after going through the material in SSME1.

		0	1	2	3	4	5	6
	0	7.01%	6.50%	4.50%	3.02%	1.31%	0.23%	0.11%
	1	9.64%	10.72%	7.41%	2.79%	1.37%	0.46%	0.11%
	2	8.72%	8.04%	5.47%	1.77%	0.34%	0.17%	0.06%
	3	4.05%	5.13%	2.11%	0.74%	0.23%	0.00%	0.00%
	4	2.28%	1.77%	0.97%	0.40%	0.00%	0.06%	0.00%
Observed	5	1.08%	0.63%	0.11%	0.06%	0.11%	0.00%	0.00%
Actual	6	0.06%	0.29%	0.11%	0.06%	0.00%	0.00%	0.00%
Frequencies	7	0	0	0	0	0	0	0
	8	0	0	0	0	0	0	0
	9	0	0	0	0	0	0	0
	10	0	0	0	0	0	0	0
	11	0	0	0	0	0	0	0
	12	0	0	0	0	0	0	0
	13	0	0	0	0	0	0	0
	14	0	0	0	0	0	0	0
	15	0	0	0	0	0	0	0

Finally, in the 3rd matrix we apply an adjustment to each exact score possibility by dividing the observed frequency of each exact score by the hypothetical frequency. This gives us a percentage adjustment we can use when we try to estimate the expected goals for a given matchup.

		0	1	2	3	4	5	6
	0	0.950687	0.8472175	0.9919576	1.5039943	1.7745927	0.9555713	1.630127
	1	0.9129453	0.9765029	1.1408669	0.9718339	1.2942188	1.33573	1.1393235
	2	1.1007112	0.9753459	1.1219841	0.8188069	0.4308951	0.6670737	0.7586491
	3	0.9743058	1.1875095	0.8248447	0.6549651	0.5479429	0	0
	4	1.3357229	0.9953498	0.9222292	0.8582075	0	1.0321125	0
Zero	5	1.8500183	1.0298471	0.3163632	0.357487	1.9439757	0	0
Inflated	6	0.3271533	1.5728199	1.062955	1.2011278	0	0	0
Adjustment	7	0	0	0	0	0	0	0
Values	8	0	0	0	0	0	0	0
	9	0	0	0	0	0	0	0
	10	0	0	0	0	0	0	0
	11	0	0	0	0	0	0	0
	12	0	0	0	0	0	0	0
	13	0	0	0	0	0	0	0
	14	0	0	0	0	0	0	0
	15	0	0	0	0	0	0	0

After having briefly walked through the process for zero inflating the negative binomial distribution to make it more appropriate for our EPL data, we're now ready to reverse engineer EPL expected goals using market prices. We can then take these implied goals for home and away teams and try to use them to get a forecast for the exact score of a game.

REMOVE VIG & ESTIMATE EXPECTED GOALS

Let's head over to the "Remove Vig & Estimate xG" sheet. As the name suggests, we're finally ready to enter 1X2 market prices for our Leicester vs Manchester game and estimate the exact score.

Market prices for home, away and draw are entered into cells E21, E22 and E23 respectively. For this game we have Leicester at 5.52, Manchester at 1.58 and a draw at 4.55 decimal odds. After that it's time to strip out the bookmaker's commission to get the no-vig implied probabilities for the game. We'll be using the logarithmic vig removal method outlined in SSME1 for this, found on the sheet starting in row 26.

20	ESTIMATED xGOALS		TEAM	NEGBIN	ODDS	NO VIG	SQ ERROR	SSE
21	HOME	AWAY	HOME	17.56%	5.520	17.10%	2.112E-05	9.87731E-05
22	0.81	1.56	AWAY	62.80%	1.580	62.32%	2.302E-05	
23			DRAW	21.62%	4.550	20.88%	5.463E-05	
24	Exponent							
25	1.0337							
26	LOG VIG REMOVAL							
27		ODDS	VIG	NO VIG	NO VIG %			
28	HOME	5.520	18.12%	5.847	17.10%			
29	AWAY	1.580	63.29%	1.605	62.32%			
30	DRAW	4.550	21.98%	4.788	20.88%			
31		Total Prob	103.39%		100.31%			

Open Solver in Excel and set the objective to cell E31, "to a value of" 1, by changing cell A25. This will adjust the log exponent in cell A25 until the estimated no-vig probabilities for this game in cells E28, E29 and E30 sum to 100%. Set the solving method to "GRG Nonlinear" and click “Solve”. When Solver is finished, cell E31 should be showing a value of 100%.

24	Exponent				
25	1.0372				
26	LOG VIG REMOVAL				
27		ODDS	VIG	NO VIG	NO VIG %
28	HOME	5.520	18.12%	5.882	17.00%
29	AWAY	1.580	63.29%	1.607	62.22%
30	DRAW	4.550	21.98%	4.814	20.77%
31		Total Prob	103.39%		100.00%

Now we need to use Solver again to estimate each team’s expected goals for this game using our newly acquired no-vig probabilities. Click “Solver” again and set the objective to H21, “to minimize (min)”, by changing cells A22 and B22. This will attempt to find the expected goals for each team that would result in our calculated no-vig probabilities. Set the solving method to “GRG nonlinear” again and click “Solve”. When Solver is complete the estimated goals for home and away will be found in cells A22 and B22.

20	ESTIMATED xGOALS		TEAM	NEGBIN	ODDS	NO VIG	SQ ERROR	SSE
21	HOME	AWAY	HOME	17.54%	5.520	17.00%	2.932E-05	0.000136873
22	0.81	1.56	AWAY	62.79%	1.580	62.22%	3.193E-05	
23			DRAW	21.64%	4.550	20.77%	7.563E-05	
24	Exponent							
25	1.0372							

Solver isn’t always able to find a perfect solution, but usually gets pretty close. You can see here that while there are some minor discrepancies between the “No-Vig” probabilities and the “NegBin” probabilities, Solver has calculated Leicester’s expected goals for this game to be 0.81 and Manchester’s to be 1.56. Now we can use this information to estimate exact score probabilities.

CALCULATE EXACT SCORE PROBABILITIES

We now open the "Probability Outputs" sheet and can observe the expected exact score probabilities for this game. These probabilities come from the negative binomial matrix in the "Remove Vig & Estimate xG" sheet. We can see that the four most likely outcomes were 1-0, 2-0, 3-0 for Manchester City or a 0-0 draw. As mentioned before, the final game score ended up being a 1-0 victory for Manchester City, which was our most likely exact score outcome at 16.24%.

EXACT SCORE			
Rank	HOME	AWAY	Probability
4	0	0	10.62%
1	0	1	16.24%
2	0	2	15.36%
3	0	3	11.77%
7	0	4	4.92%
18	0	5	0.70%
8	1	0	4.06%
5	1	1	7.45%
6	1	2	7.03%
11	1	3	3.02%
14	1	4	1.43%
20	1	5	0.39%
12	2	0	2.22%
9	2	1	3.38%
10	2	2	3.14%

Most Likely Scores			
Rank	Home	Away	Probability
1	0	1	16.24%
2	0	2	15.36%
3	0	3	11.77%
4	0	0	10.62%

Obviously, we won't always be able to hit the nail right on the head like this, but reverse engineering a forecast in this manner can be a useful tool for helping to inform exact score betting strategies.

---

1. Of course, this is the frequentist approach. Doing some reading about Bayesian statistical modelling will probably convince you that what we actually want in most cases is a range of outcomes rather than a single point estimate.
2. https://www.football-data.co.uk/data.php
3. The Conway-Maxwell Poisson distribution is likely to be a better fit here, but the negative binomial provides a nice example while keeping things relatively simple. You may also want to try using a zero inflated Poisson distribution instead. See http://www.opisthokonta.net/?p=1157 for more information.
4. Please refer to the Statistical Sports Models in Excel Volume 1 chapter on EPL model ideas for more information.

PROP MODELS

12

NFL PASSING YARDS

It's difficult to know exactly how many yards a quarterback might throw for in a given game. However, despite the fact that we might not know precisely, we can use simulations to approximate a solution by focusing on what we *are* be able to know - the distribution of the uncertainty.

Question: how many passing yards will Jimmy Garoppolo throw for in this year's Super Bowl?

Let's take a look at how we might try to arrive at a decent estimate for this type of player prop bet using a Monte Carlo simulation in Excel.

STEP 1: BRAINSTORM A FORMULA

Props are all about opportunity and efficiency. Find a way to reasonably address those two elements and most of the time you've arrived at a decent solution to your modelling challenge. First we need to decide how to organize the components of this prop bet that we'll want to account for. You might consider this step as brainstorming for sources of outcome variance. We can start from the reasonable position that passing yards in the NFL are a function of at least a few things:

---

1. The expected passing yards per pass attempt of the quarterback
2. The expected number of passing plays attempted
3. The opposing pass defense

In theory, if we can get decent estimates of these 3 elements we should be able to put them together like this:

Passing Yards = (yards per attempt) * (# of pass plays) * (defense)

So say for example we expect a quarterback to have a yards per attempt [Y/A] efficiency of 7.7, 32 total passing plays attempted, and an opponent pass defense adjustment compared to league average of 1 (or exactly league average). Our hypothetical quarterback would be expected to perform as follows:

Passing Yards = (7.7) * (32) * (1)

= 246.4 yards

This single point estimate looks alright, but we'll want to additionally account for the small sample size and high variance of an NFL season. For that, we'll use a Monte Carlo simulation - and in order to do so effectively we first need to understand how our input variables behave.

STEP 2: ESTIMATE INPUT DISTRIBUTIONS

With our general model blueprint roughly mapped out, we next collect a sample for each of our data inputs and observe how they generally behave using some form of distribution fitting software. You can do this using the Easy Fit distribution fitting Excel add-on that was discussed in SSME1, or with more expensive Excel add-ons like Solver's optimization upgrade package.

Whatever distribution add-on we use, we'll likely end up with similar distribution suggestions so I'll go ahead and walk you through what I found in my tests.[1] After gathering quarterback pass attempt and yards per attempt data from the 2019 NFL regular season and fitting it, the Uniform distribution and the Weibull distribution appeared to be the best fit for pass attempts and yards per attempt respectively. This is good news, because these two distributions are relatively simple to simulate in Excel. Let's go over how to do that now.

STEP 3: ESTIMATING PARAMETERS

Let's open up the "QB Passing Yards" Excel file. You'll see we have inputs for pass yards per attempt in column A and pass attempts in column F. Our first task is to estimate the parameters of the Weibull distribution using maximum likelihood estimation.[2]

A	B	C	D	E	F	G	H	I
Weibull Fitting		Weibull Parameters			Uniform Fitting	Uniform Parameters		
Y/A	Log Likelihood	ALPHA (SIZE)	9.512160794		Attempts	MIN	20	
5.22	3.294760623	BETA (SHAPE)	3.088634339		27	MAX	46	
12.44	2.97465349	N	16		25	N	16	
6.47	3.595731536	MLE	-39.7891924		32			
7.62	3.737480559				29			
6	3.501407503				33			
5.05	3.240840262				21			
7.73	3.744600603				22			
10.73	3.505648768				37			
4.85	3.173038945				46			
9.2	3.733031982				45			
14.65	1.811048159				20			
8.81	3.755521743				21			
10.97	3.449265519				35			
6.47	3.595731536				34			
6.59	3.616353739				27			
12.95	2.755921491				22			
SUM	53.48503646							

All of the data in this sheet comes from pro-football-reference.com. We start by taking Jimmy Garoppolo's regular season net yards per pass attempt data and inputting it into cells A3 to A18. Next, we use Solver to estimate the size and shape of the Weibull distribution for Garoppolo's yards per pass attempt data (alpha & beta in cells D2/D3). Click on Solver and enter the following:

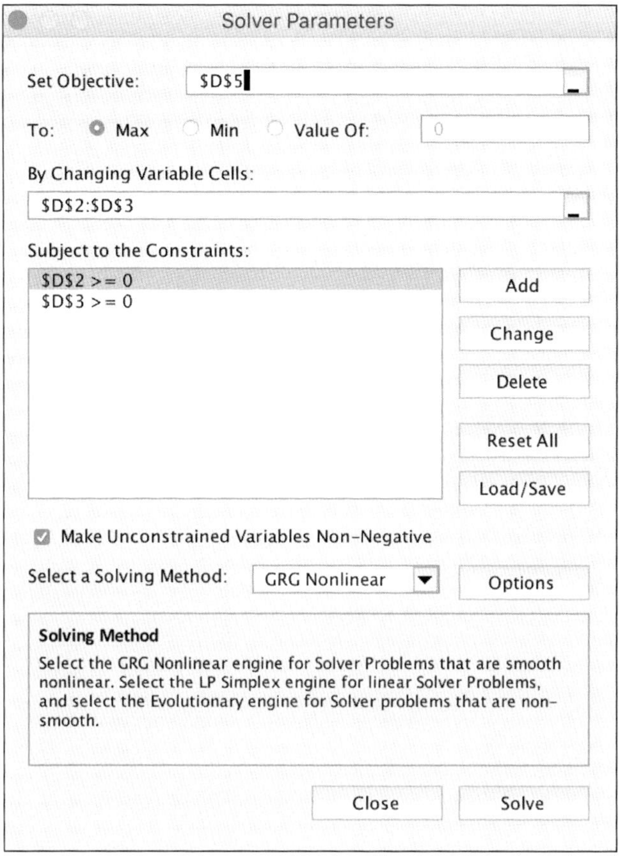

What we're doing here is asking Solver to adjust the size and shape parameters of our Weibull distribution until the log likelihood is maximized. Click "Solve" and when Solver is finished you'll see that the estimated parameters for Garoppolo's pass yards per attempt are 9.512 for size in cell D2 and 3.088 for shape in cell D3.

C	D
Weibull Parameters	
ALPHA (SIZE)	9.512160794
BETA (SHAPE)	3.088634339
N	16
MLE	-39.7891924

With our Weibull distribution now fitted it's time to move on to our Uniform distribution for expected pass attempts. This task is quite simple - we input Garoppolo's pass attempt data from the regular season into cells F3 to F18 and the sheet automatically calculates the minimum and maximum values in cells H2/H3. Easy breezy.

F	G	H
Uniform Fitting	Uniform Parameters	
Attempts	MIN	20
27	MAX	46
25	N	16
32		
29		
33		
21		
22		
37		
46		
45		
20		
21		
35		
34		
27		
22		

Next, we add an opponent defense adjustment in row 22. Garoppolo is up against the Kansas City Chiefs, so we input the Chief's yards per pass attempt against value (5.7) into cell B22. Then we input the league average yards per pass attempt against value into cell C22. The sheet then calculates a percentage adjustment value of 0.905 in cell D22.

21	Opp	Y/A Against	League Average	Def ADJ%
22	KAN	5.7	6.3	0.904761905
23				

We now have all the components we need to build our simulation.

SIMULATING PASSING YARDS

The sheet can now estimate Garoppolo's passing yards using the simulated values in columns J to L. Every time you press the "delete" key in an empty cell, the simulation will run again. Column J simulates Garoppolo's yards per pass attempt using the Weibull parameters we fitted earlier with the following formula:

```
=$D$2*(-LN(1-RAND()))^(1/$D$3)
```

Column K simulates Garoppolo's pass attempts using our Uniform distribution parameters with the following formula:

```
=RAND()*($H$3-$H$2)+$H$2
```

Column L is the opponent adjustment percentage taken from cell D22. In column M, we then multiply the simulated values together using our basic model formula from the start of this chapter:

Passing Yards = (yards per attempt) * (# of pass plays) * (defense)

This produces the desired passing yard estimates. As a final step, we drag/populate the simulation down to row 1002 to simulate this particular game 1,000 times.

J	K	L	M
MONTE CARLO SIMULATION			
Yards/Attempt Sim	Pass Attempt Sim	Defense ADJ%	Simulated Pass Yards
7.28	40.99	0.9048	269.97
5.65	32.43	0.9048	165.86
7.27	24.21	0.9048	159.35
2.87	36.79	0.9048	95.64
11.75	25.74	0.9048	273.58
8.25	25.77	0.9048	192.35
7.42	26.42	0.9048	177.32
9.32	26.01	0.9048	219.42

MAKING PREDICTIONS

Columns N through X are the functions for estimating the probability of Garoppolo going over or under his posted prop line. For this particular prop, the passing yards line was 237.5 (inputted into cell R2). In column N, we use an IF function to record the number of times in our 1,000 simulated games that Garoppolo passed for more than 237.5 yards. A value of "1" in column N denotes that the total passing yards in that individual simulation was over the posted line, while "0" denotes that the total passing yards was under.

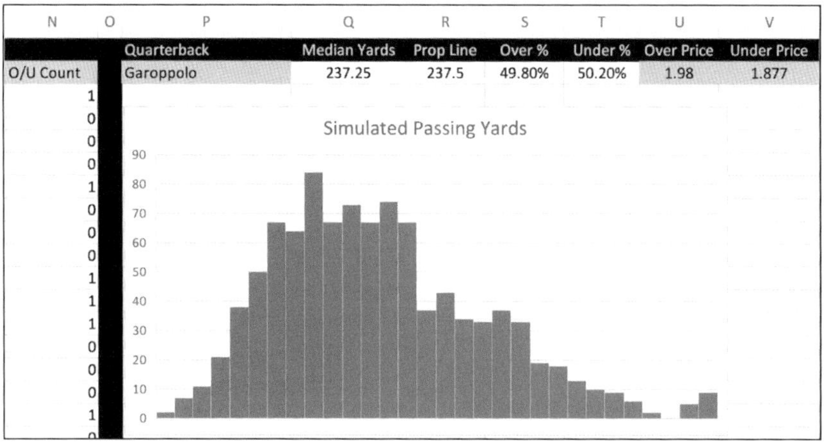

In cells S2 and T2 we then use a COUNTIF function calculate the percentage of times in our 1,000 simulations that Garoppolo went over or under the 237.5 prop line for passing yards. Don't worry if your results look slightly different than what is pictured above - remember, the simulation refreshes every time you hit a key in a blank cell. In the pictured simulation, we can see that the market line was right on the money - we have a simulated expectation that Garoppolo will throw for 237.25 yards. Given that this is not significantly different from the posted line of 237.5, we unsurprisingly see that there is little value on either side of this passing yards prop in cells W2 and X2.

Jimmy Garoppolo ended up passing for 219 yards.

IMPROVEMENTS

There are few things we could do to improve upon what we've built so far. First, we might want to try some different distributions. Second, we may want to take into account the expected spread of the game. Teams that are losing in a game situation tend to throw the ball more, and we might be able to incorporate that information into our simulation to improve its accuracy. Finally, we might want to account for the variation in opponent defense. It's unlikely that Kansas would always play to their average defensive efficiency - so incorporating that into our simulation might further help us map the uncertainty of passing yard results. I leave these as suggestions for you to explore.

---

1. These are decent distributions to start with. You may wish to experiment on your own as well.
2. The technical details of the method that follows can be found at Charles Zaiontz's website: http://www.real-statistics.com/distribution-fitting/distribution-fitting-via-maximum-likelihood/fitting-weibull-parameters-mle/

13

NBA REBOUNDS

How many total rebounds [TRB] will Andre Drummond get tonight against the Miami Heat for their February 24th, 2020 matchup?

Let's find out together with a basic model for estimating player rebounds in the NBA. Open the "NBA Rebounds" Excel file to follow along with this chapter.

BASIC MODEL STRUCTURE

Just like we did with QB passing yards, we'll want to brainstorm a model structure here that roughly captures the major sources of variation in player performance. When it comes to NBA rebounding, for our purposes those sources of variation are:

---

1. Player expected minutes
2. Player expected rebounds per minute
3. Opponent rebounding "defense"

There are much more intricate ways to model rebounding, but this should be a good starting point. If we get a decent handle on these 3 elements, we'll be in good shape to make a reasonable estimate for a given player. One way to structure a model with these elements would be:

TRB = Expected Minutes * Expected TRB/Min * Opp ADJ%

So for example, if Drummond was expected to get 26 minutes tonight at an expected rate of 0.44 TRB per minute against a league average team for rebound defence (a value of 1.00), the calculation would look like this:

Drummond TRB = 26 * 0.44 * 1.00

Drummond TRB = 11.44

That's pretty straightforward. Now we just need to get the components for the model together.

PLAYER MINUTES

The data we're looking for can be found at basketball-reference.com. Once we arrive at the website, we search for "Andre Drummond" in the search bar in the top right corner of the landing page.

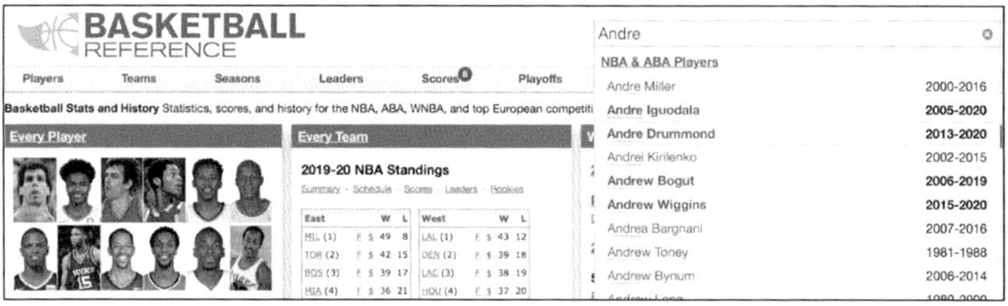

Once we click on Andre's name in the search bar, we're taken to Drummond's player page. From here, we want to click on his 2019-2020 game logs.

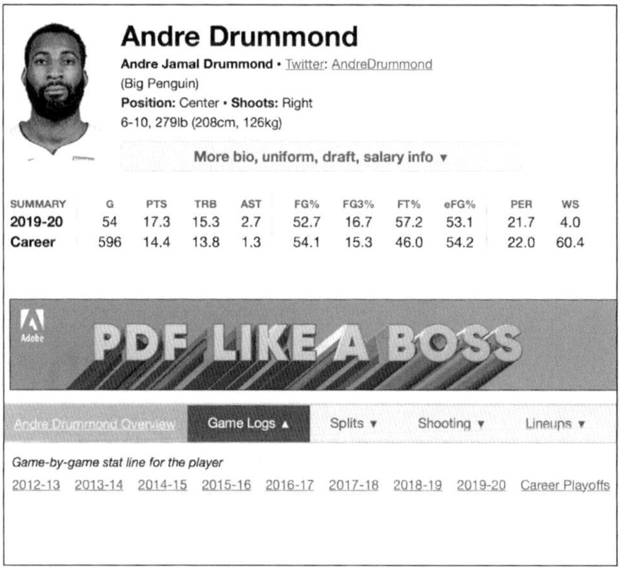

We we click on "2019-2020" under "Game Logs", we finally arrive at Drummond's game data - which contains his minutes and stat production performance game by game. This is the data we'll want to copy and paste into the "2. Player Logs" sheet of our Excel file.

2019-20 Regular Season Share & more ▾ Glossary

Rk	G	Date ▲	Age	Tm		Opp		GS	MP	FG	FGA	FG%	3P	3PA	3P%	FT	FTA	FT%	ORB	DRB	TRB	AST	STL	BLK	TOV	PF	PTS	GmSc	+/-
1	1	2019-10-23	26-074	DET	@	IND	W (+9)	1	40:48	12	18	.667	0	1	.000	8	10	.800	7	16	23	2	3	4	2	4	32	36.7	+4
2	2	2019-10-24	26-075	DET		ATL	L (-17)	1	36:45	8	12	.667	0	0		5	6	.833	1	11	12	2	4	1	4	4	21	19.9	-15
3	3	2019-10-26	26-077	DET		PHI	L (-6)	1	24:38	5	10	.500	0	0		3	10	.300	3	9	12	1	0	2	2	6	13	7.7	-1
4	4	2019-10-28	26-079	DET		IND	W (+2)	1	38:18	8	15	.533	0	1	.000	2	3	.667	4	14	18	1	0	2	6	3	18	12.2	+3
5	5	2019-10-30	26-081	DET	@	TOR	L (-12)	1	35:20	10	17	.588	0	0		1	2	.500	8	14	22	3	0	1	5	4	21	18.7	-22
6	6	2019-11-01	26-083	DET	@	CHI	L (-6)	1	35:06	11	17	.647	0	2	.000	3	5	.600	6	18	24	2	2	3	5	4	25	25.2	-8
7	7	2019-11-02	26-084	DET		BRK	W (+4)	1	38:51	10	16	.625	0	1	.000	5	6	.833	3	17	20	6	3	5	4	4	25	29.7	+8
8	8	2019-11-04	26-086	DET	@	WAS	L (-16)	1	38:49	6	20	.300	0	1	.000	3	3	1.000	8	16	24	4	2	2	4	5	15	14.0	-5
9	9	2019-11-06	26-088	DET		NYK	W (+20)	1	34:54	12	16	.750	0	0		3	4	.750	4	8	12	7	1	0	4	1	27	26.9	+24
10	10	2019-11-08	26-090	DET	@	IND	L (-6)	1	33:36	6	14	.429	0	2	.000	3	4	.750	1	12	13	8	0	1	4	5	15	11.8	+9

Let's copy and paste this data into our sheet and head back to Excel. There is a lot we could analyze within this dataset, but for now we'll focus on the model inputs we're interested in - namely minutes and TRB per minute.

We start by deleting any rows in the dataset where Drummond didn't play. Then, in column AF of our "Player Logs" sheet, we transform minutes to a purely numeric value so that they're a bit easier to work with. This means that we'll convert 27 minutes and 39 seconds to a value of 27.65 for example. We do this in column AF using the following formula:

```
=(TEXT(J2,"[mm]"))/60
```

We then drag/populate this formula down all the rows in the dataset. In column AG we calculate the TRB per minute efficiency that Drummond recorded in every game that he played. This calculation is simply TRB divided by our new minutes played variable in column AF. Finally, in cell AH2 we calculate the frequency that Drummond fouls out of games. Players that have higher rates of fouling out have a greater chance of underperforming their expectations, so this is always a handy thing to note.

AB	AC	AD	AE	AF	AG	AH
PTS	GmSc	+/-		Minutes Played	Rebounds Per Minute	Foul Out Percentage
32	36.7	4		40.80	0.564	9.43%
21	19.9	-15		36.75	0.327	
13	7.7	-1		24.63	0.487	
18	12.2	3		38.30	0.470	
21	18.7	-22		35.33	0.623	
25	25.2	-8		35.10	0.684	
25	29.7	8		38.85	0.515	
15	14	-5		38.82	0.618	
27	26.9	24		34.90	0.344	
15	11.8	9		33.60	0.387	

This is accomplished using an COUNTIF function in Excel where we calculate the percentage of games that Drummond had 6 fouls.

Heading back to the dashboard, you'll see that we've calculated Drummond's median minutes per game over the season in cell B2 and his median minutes for the last 3 games in cell D2. We have also calculated the standard deviation of his minutes in cell F2.

A	B	C	D
Player	Median Minutes	Median TRB/Min	Last 3 MIN
Andre Drummond	=MEDIAN('2. Player Game Logs'!$AF$2:$AF$54)		

That should be all we need to know about player minutes, so let's calculate the TRB data we need next.

TOTAL REBOUNDS PER MINUTE

In cells C2, E2 and G2 of the main dashboard we calculate the median TRB/min for the season, the median TRB/min for the last 3 games and the TRB/min standard deviation respectively.

OPPONENT TRB DEFENCE ADJUSTMENT

For our opponent adjustment percentage, we divide Miami's TRB against per game stat from basketball-reference.com by the league average. In the main 2019-2020 NBA season summary page of basketball-reference.com, we can see that Miami's TRB against is on average 42.2 while the league average is 45. We enter these values into cells A5 and B5 on the main dashboard of our sheet and the calculated adjustment value of 0.9378 appears in cell C5. This is the value we'll use to adjust Drummond's expected TRB production.

PUTTING IT ALL TOGETHER

For the sake of simplicity, we'll proceed on the basis that both minutes and TRB per minute are normally distributed. This isn't necessarily the perfect distribution fit for our data, but it's close enough that we should still be able to produce a reasonable estimate of player performance. Should you wish to investigate more nuanced possibilities, consider a Weibull or Logistic distribution.

Now that we have all of our model components together we can create a simulation of 1,000 games and see what Andre Drummond's performance expectations should be. We do this by simulating minutes and TRB/min using the NORM.INV function in Excel. This is similar to the 3 point competition Monte Carlo simulation we ran in SSME1, but this time we are also adding player minutes and an opponent adjustment - both of which were unnecessary for the 3 point competition.

Minutes are simulated in column I using the following formula:

```
=NORM.INV(RAND(),(0.6*$D$2+0.4*$B$2),$F$2)
```

You'll notice that what we're doing here is weighting Drummond's minutes so that his season median carries a weight of 40% and his last 3 games carry a weight of 60%.

Next, TRB/min is simulated in column J using the following formula:

=NORM.INV(RAND(),(0.6*$E$2+0.4*$C$2),$G$2)

Again here, we are using the same 40%/60% weighting for the season median and last 3 games median.

C	D	E	F	G	H	I	J	K	L	
Median TRB/Min	Last 3 MIN	Last 3 TRB/Min	STDEV Min	STDEV TRB/MIN		MIN SIM	TRB/MIN SIM	OPP DEF ADJ%	xTRB	O/
0.470	22.13	0.549	6.125	0.111		36.61	=NORM.INV(RAND(),(0.6*$E$2+0.4*$C$2),$G$2)			
						24.55	0.448	1.0611	11.67	
						29.73	0.544	1.0611	17.16	
						35.55	0.461	1.0611	17.37	
						24.26	0.429	1.0611	11.03	
						23.37	0.654	1.0611	16.20	
						32.26	0.584	1.0611	19.98	
						15.01	0.408	1.0611	6.49	

Finally, in column L we multiply the simulated minutes and TRB/min together and then multiply the result by the opponent adjustment percentage to get an expected number of total rebounds.

H	I	J	K	L	M
	MIN SIM	TRB/MIN SIM	OPP DEF ADJ%	xTRB	O/U
	13.90	0.575	1.0611	=I2*J2*K2	0
	41.84	0.585	1.0611	26.00	1
	40.81	0.588	1.0611	25.44	1
	19.98	0.370	1.0611	7.84	0
	25.76	0.592	1.0611	16.19	1
	41.24	0.682	1.0611	29.84	1

MAKING PREDICTIONS

Every time you press the "delete" key in a blank cell, the simulation will refresh. Columns M through W are the functions for estimating the probability of Andre Drummond going over or under his posted TRB prop line. For this particular prop, the TRB line was 13.5 (inputted into cell Q2). In column M, we use an IF function to record the number of times in our 1,000 simulated games that Drummond had more than 13.5 rebounds. A value of "1" in column M denotes that the TRB value in that individual simulation was over the posted line, while "0" denotes that the TRB value was under.

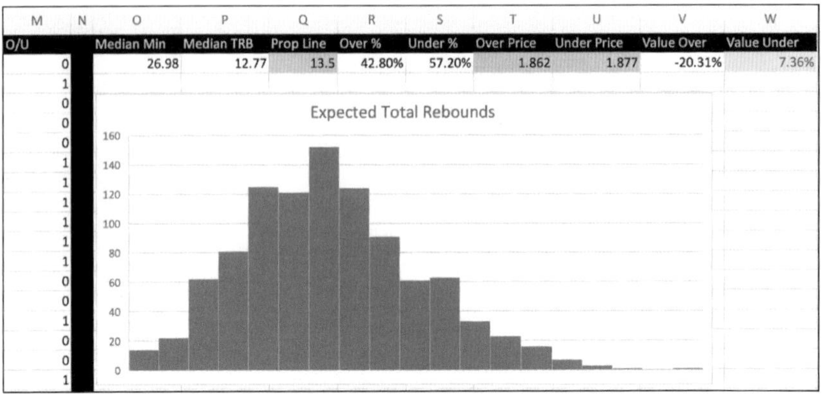

In cells R2 and S2 we then use a COUNTIF function calculate the percentage of times in our 1,000 simulations that Drummond went over or under the 13.5 TRB prop line. Don't worry if your results look slightly different than what is pictured above - remember, the simulation refreshes every time you hit a key in a blank cell. In the pictured simulation, we can see that there appears to be value on the under.

Andrew Drummond ended up playing 24 minutes and had 6 rebounds, a far cry from his performances in Detroit prior to being traded to Cleveland. Changes in his usage and minutes were reflected in his most recent games - and we were able to weight our simulation to roughly model that.

14

MLB PITCHER STRIKEOUTS

The first two player prop models we've looked at have used Monte Carlo simulations, so in this chapter I'd like to walk you through a regression based model to show you a different method for estimating player performance. This particular model deals with pitcher strikeouts (K's) in the MLB. I discussed the broad strokes of this model on a podcast[1] earlier this year with Benjamin Cronin[2] of Pinnacle Sports, but here we'll go a bit more in-depth and try to make it more fully functional. Open the "MLB Pitchers Strikes" Excel file to follow along with this chapter.

A	B	C	D	E
PITCHER	Strike %	Looking Strike %	Swinging Strike %	Foul Strike %
Walker Buehler	68.60%	26.90%	19.80%	28.80%
Base Expectation	Opponent ADJ	Adjusted Expectation	Expected IP/G	Expected BF/IP
28.01%	1.0379	29.08%	6.16	4.02
xK% = -0.8432 + (Str% * 0.2916) + (L/Str * 1.2689) + (S/Str * 1.5334) + (F/Str * 0.9672)				
xK = Adjusted Expectation * xIP/G * xBF/IP				

BASIC MODEL STRUCTURE

When brainstorming how to solve a sports modelling problem, we start by imagining the ideal scenario. Once we have some idea of the pieces or components we'd ideally want to know to be able to predict player performance, we can begin trying to collect them using various statistical methods.

So in an ideal scenario, what would we need to know to make a prediction about how many strikeouts a pitcher (Walker Buehler in this instance) will get in a given game?

The following seems like a good starting point for model components:

The pitchers strikeout %

The opponent strikeout %

The total number of batters faced per inning

The number of innings pitched

If we could get reasonable numbers of each of these elements, we'd probably have a pretty good idea how many strikeouts Buehler would have in any given game. Then, we could put the model components together like this:

K's = Strikeout % * Opp ADJ% * IP * BF/IP

So for example, if Buehler has a strikeout percentage of 28.01%, facing an opponent that strikes out 103.79% of league average, and we expect Buehler to pitch 6.16 innings and face 4.20 batters per inning, our forecast would look like this:

K's = 28.01% * 1.0379 * 6.61 * 4.20

K's = 7.20

That seems like a pretty reasonable process. Let's begin gathering the components we need to make it happen.

PITCHER STRIKEOUT RATE

Let's head over to baseball-reference.com and get some data on Walker Buehler. Since we're currently in-between seasons, we'll use data from last year. We start by searching for Buehler's name in the search bar.

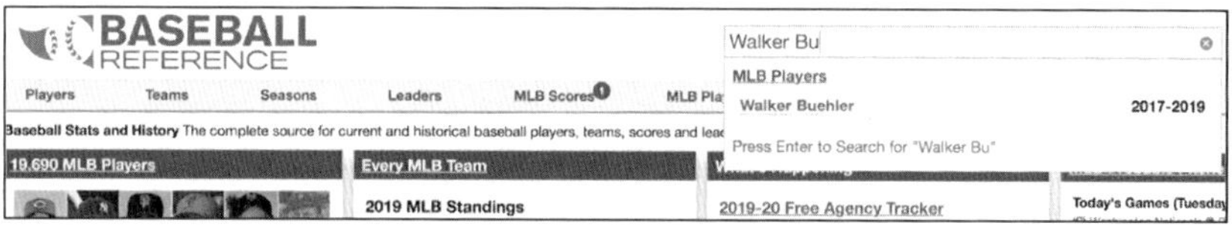

We then go to Buehler's player page and select his 2019 pitching log.

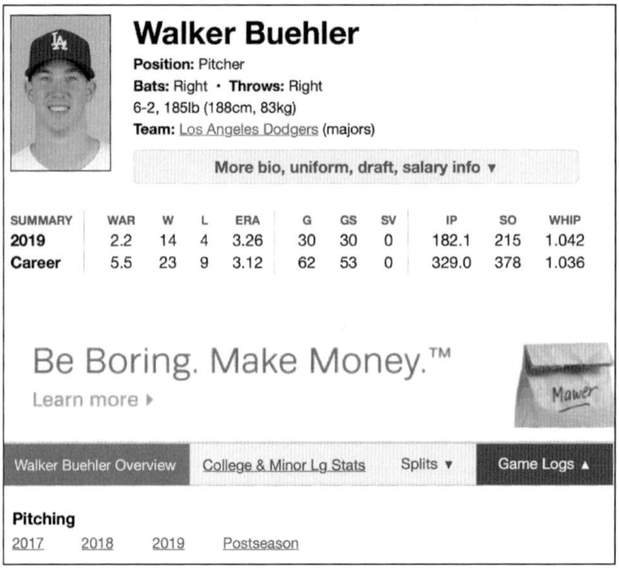

When we arrive at the game log, we copy and paste the strikeout (SO) data from the log into our dashboard sheet in column F.

2019 Pitching Game Log

Click two rows to sum games (Clear) Click pitches for details from BrooksBaseball.net Share & more ▾ Glossary

Rk	Gcar	Gtm	Date ▲	Tm		Opp	Rslt	Inngs	Dec	DR	IP	H	R	ER	BB	SO	HR	HBP	ERA	BF	Pit	Str	StL
1	33	4	Mar 31	LAD		ARI	W,8-7	GS-4		99	3.0	5	5	5	1	0	0	0	15.00	15	66	45	10
2	34	9	Apr 6	LAD	@	COL	W,7-2	GS-5	W(1-0)	5	5.0	3	1	1	2	4	1	0	6.75	19	79	50	14
3	35	14	Apr 11	LAD	@	STL	L,7-11	GS-4		4	4.0	5	5	5	2	5	0	1	8.25	20	85	51	15
4	36	20	Apr 17	LAD		CIN	W,3-2	GS-7	W(2-0)	5	6.1	3	1	0	1	8	0	0	5.40	22	92	57	18
5	37	26	Apr 24	LAD	@	CHC	L,6-7	GS-6		6	5.2	4	3	3	2	1	1	0	5.25	22	96	55	14
6	38	32	Apr 30	LAD	@	SFG	W,10-3	GS-6	W(3-0)	5	5.1	6	3	3	1	6	0	0	5.22	22	95	66	18
7	39	37	May 6	LAD		ATL	W,5-3	GS-7	W(4-0)	5	7.0	5	3	3	0	8	2	0	4.95	26	100	74	26
8	40	42	May 11	LAD		WSN	L,2-5	GS-7		4	7.0	4	0	0	1	7	0	0	4.15	25	97	66	19
9	41	47	May 18	LAD	@	CIN	L,0-4	GS-6	L(4-1)	6	6.0	7	4	1	0	7	1	0	3.83	26	99	71	10

We'll use this data to estimate the variance of Buehler's strikeout distribution later. In the meantime though, we want to click on Buehler's advanced pitching stats and retrieve his strike %, swinging strike %, looking strike % and foul strike %.

Walker Buehler Overview | College & Minor Lg Stats | Splits ▾ | Game Logs ▾ | Finders & Advanced Stats ▴

Pitching

Advanced Stats Home Run Log Game Finder Streak Finder Event Finder vs. Batter Pitcher Comparison Postseason

Batting

Advanced Stats Home Run Log Game Finder Streak Finder Event Finder vs. Pitcher Batter Comparison Postseason

Fielding

Advanced Stats

Pitch Summary -- Pitching * Share & more ▾ Glossary

Year	Age	Tm	Lg	PA	Pit	Pit/PA	Str	Str%	L/Str	S/Str	F/Str	I/Str	AS/Str	I/Bll	AS/Pit
2017	22	LAD	NL	44	192	4.36	119	62.0%	29.4%	18.5%	31.9%	20.2%	70.6%	0.0%	43.8%
2018	23	LAD	NL	543	2173	4.00	1458	67.1%	26.9%	18.7%	30.7%	23.8%	73.1%	0.0%	49.1%
2019	24	LAD	NL	739	2838	3.84	1939	68.3%	26.4%	19.8%	29.2%	24.7%	73.6%	0.0%	50.3%
3 Yrs				**1326**	**5203**	**3.92**	**3516**	**67.6%**	**26.7%**	**19.3%**	**29.9%**	**24.1%**	**73.3%**	**0.0%**	**49.5%**
MLB Averages						**3.90**		**63.7%**	**26.2%**	**18.4%**	**28.0%**	**27.4%**	**73.8%**	**0.0%**	**47.0%**

It appears that Buehler's strike % stats for 2019 were as follows:

Strike % = 68.3%

Looking Strike % = 26.4%

Swinging Strike % = 19.8%

Foul Strike % = 29.2%

These are the regression input variables that we need. We then plug them into Mike Podhorzer's[3] xK% regression equation from FanGraphs[4]:

xK% = -0.8432 + (Str% * 0.2916) + (L/Str * 1.2689) + (S/Str * 1.5334) + (F/Str * 0.9672)

Adjusted R-Squared: 0.931

Image Source: https://fantasy.fangraphs.com/introducing-the-new-pitcher-xk-updated-for-2017/

The strike % input variables are all entered manually into the main dashboard sheet in the labelled cells, and then the regression is calculated automatically. Once that is complete, Buehler's base expected strikeout rate (27.68%) is found in cell A4.

	A
1	PITCHER
2	Walker Buehler
3	Base Expectation
4	27.68%
5	

OPPONENT STRIKEOUT ADJUSTMENT

The opponent strikeout % adjustment is made by dividing the opposing team's strikeout % by the league average strikeout %. We can get this information from Fangraphs.com again, under team batting.

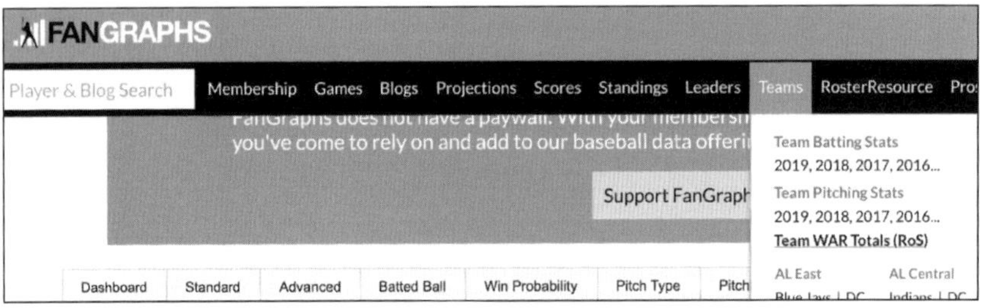

We then divide the K% rate of the opposing team by the league average to derive a percentage adjustment value for Buehler's strikeout rate. Let's suppose that the opposing team in this scenario is the San Francisco Giants.

Show Filters | Custom Reports — Export Data

Page size: 30 — 30 items in 1 pages

#	Team	PA	BB%+	K%+	AVG+	OBP+	SLG+	wRC+	ISO+	BABIP+	LD+%	GB%+	FB%+	Pull%+	Cent%+	Oppo%+	SO	K%
1	Astros	6394	119	80	108	109	113	125	119	99	101	98	102	103	101	94	1166	18.2 %
2	Twins	6392	97	91	106	104	112	116	120	101	104	91	108	105	97	96	1334	20.9 %
3	Yankees	6245	107	101	105	105	111	117	119	103	99	99	102	99	101	101	1437	23.0 %
4	Dodgers	6281	109	99	100	102	106	111	115	97	101	94	106	102	99	98	1356	21.6 %
5	Red Sox	6475	107	93	106	105	106	106	105	105	98	101	100	97	101	104	1382	21.3 %
6	Nationals	6267	105	95	103	103	102	103	101	102	97	97	105	103	95	101	1308	20.9 %
7	Braves	6302	111	106	100	102	102	102	104	102	109	95	101	103	94	103	1467	23.3 %
8	Cubs	6195	106	108	98	100	102	102	107	99	93	107	96	97	101	103	1460	23.6 %
9	Rockies	6288	88	109	103	99	102	86	102	107	104	99	99	94	102	107	1503	23.9 %

Looking at the far right column (K%) we can see down at the bottom that the Giants have a team strikeout rate of 23.3%, compared to a league average of 22.98%. This tells us that the Giants should be expected to strikeout more often than average, so Buehler's base K% rate needs a slight boost. 23.3%/22.95% = 1.0137, so we enter that value into cell B4 of the sheet and Buehler's expected K% is adjusted to 28.06% in cell C4.

EXPECTED INNINGS PITCHED

Now that we have an estimate of Buehler's success rate for strikeouts in this matchup, we need an estimate for the number of chances or opportunities he will get to strike a batter out. For this we look at his standard pitching stats back on baseball-reference.com.

Standard Pitching Show Minors Share & more ▾ Glossary

Year	Age	Tm	Lg	W	L	W-L%	ERA	G	GS	GF	CG	SHO	SV	IP	H	R	ER	HR	BB	IBB	SO	HBP	BK	WP	BF
2017	22	LAD	NL	1	0	1.000	7.71	8	0	2	0	0	0	9.1	11	8	8	2	8	1	12	0	0	1	44
2018	23	LAD	NL	8	5	.615	2.62	24	23	0	0	0	0	137.1	95	43	40	12	37	1	151	6	0	4	541
2019	24	LAD	NL	14	4	**.778**	3.26	30	30	0	**2**	0	0	182.1	153	77	66	20	37	0	215	7	0	4	737
3 Yrs				**23**	**9**	**.719**	**3.12**	**62**	**53**	**2**	**2**	**0**	**0**	**329.0**	**259**	**128**	**114**	**34**	**82**	**2**	**378**	**13**	**0**	**9**	**1322**
162 Game Avg.				**14**	**5**	**.719**	**3.12**	**37**	**31**	**1**	**1**	**0**	**0**	**195**	**153**	**76**	**67**	**20**	**48**	**1**	**224**	**8**	**0**	**5**	**782**

Buehler played in 30 games and pitched for a total of 182.1 innings, giving us an average of 6.07 innings pitched per game. We enter that value into cell D4 on the sheet.

BATTERS FACED PER INNING

Looking at the same standard pitching stats as above, we see that Buehler faced 737 batters in 2019 over 182.1 innings. This gives us an average batters faced per inning pitched value of 4.05. We enter this value into cell E4.

A	B	C	D	E
PITCHER	Strike %	Looking Strike %	Swinging Strike %	Foul Strike %
Walker Buehler	68.30%	26.40%	19.80%	29.20%
Base Expectation	Opponent ADJ	Adjusted Expectation	Expected IP/G	Expected BF/IP
27.68%	1.0137	28.06%	6.07	4.05

Putting this all together, our prediction for Walker Buehler looks like this:

K's = Strikeout % * Opp ADJ% * IP * BF/IP

K's = 28.06% * 1.0137 * 6.16 * 4.02

K's = 6.95

MAKING PREDICTIONS

Now that we have a point estimate for Walker Buehler's expected number of strikeouts, we need to convert that estimate into a probability so that we can compare it to market prices for an over/under prop line.

For this task, we'll be using the negative binomial distribution we saw earlier in the EPL exact scores Excel file. The function of the distribution works exactly the same as before, only this time the mean is Buehler's expected strikeouts (6.95) and the variance is calculated from his strikeout data in column F using the VAR function in Excel.

We can use these numbers along with the negative binomial distribution to estimate the probability that Buehler strikes out a given number of batters in our hypothetical matchup against the Giants.

Pitcher K Data	Walker Buehler		Strikeout Count	PROB %	CUMUL %
0	MEAN	6.90	0	0.73%	0.73%
4	VARIANCE	13.08	1	2.64%	3.37%
5	B	0.897	2	5.43%	8.80%
8	R	7.692	3	8.30%	17.10%
1	KURTOSIS	-1.541	4	10.49%	27.59%
6	SKEW	0.101	5	11.59%	39.18%
8			6	11.59%	50.78%
7			7	10.72%	61.50%
7			8	9.31%	70.81%
6			9	7.67%	78.48%
6			10	6.06%	84.54%
11			11	4.60%	89.14%
9			12	3.39%	92.53%
6			13	2.43%	94.96%
16			14	1.70%	96.66%
4			15	1.16%	97.82%

Expected K's	Prop Line	Over %	Under %	Price Over	Price Under	Value Over	Value Under
6.90	7.5	38.50%	61.50%	1.961	1.775	-24.50%	9.16%

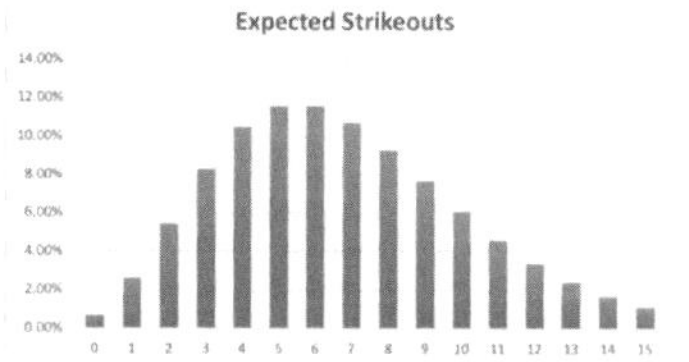

To make a prediction, we enter the prop line into cell N2, and the over/under prices into cells Q2 and R2. The model then uses the VLOOKUP function to find the cumulative probability of going under the prop line and inputs it into cell P2, subsequently calculating the probability of going over automatically as well. The line and over/under prices in this example are fictional, but you can see how they operate. If this had been an actual line, we would've see value on the under. Of course, you'll want to test this out on actual games to get a sense of how well it performs in real life.

---

1. https://soundcloud.com/pinnacle-podcast/a-guide-to-modelling-in-sports-betting
2. @PinnacleBen on Twitter.
3. Mike Podhorzer also wrote a fantastic book on baseball projections called "Projecting X 2.0". It's a recommended read.
4. https://fantasy.fangraphs.com/introducing-the-new-pitcher-xk-updated-for-2017/

BAYES & ANECDOTAL THOUGHTS

15

SIMPLE BAYESIAN APPLICATIONS

This chapter is intended to give you a quick demonstration of some different ways you can apply Bayes' Theorem to sports modelling challenges. While it is by no means comprehensive, I think what most readers are really looking for is a reason to investigate Bayesian statistical methods further. The following examples will hopefully encourage you to learn more in your search for new and useful sports modelling tools.

THE HEART OF BAYESIAN INFERENCE

What is Bayesian inference all about? Excellent explanations can be found all over the web, but I'm personally a fan of this particularly concise description on the website QuantStart[1]:

> Bayesian statistics is a particular approach to applying probability to statistical problems. It provides us with mathematical tools to update our beliefs about random events in light of seeing new data or evidence about those events.

That's the heart of Bayesian inference right there - updating our beliefs or probabilistic assessments in the face of new evidence. We already do this all the time in our everyday lives. To perform this mathematically though, we'll need the specific tool the above quoted paragraph refers to. That tool is an equation for conditional probability known as Bayes' Rule.

The standard equation structure, while fairly intuitive, doesn't necessarily make its application to sports modelling questions self-evident to the beginner.[2] Instead, there is an alternative configuration that is more helpful[3]. That transposed version of Bayes' Rule is as follows:

$$P(A|B) = \frac{P(B|A)P(A)}{\sum_{a \in A} P(B|A)P(A)}$$

Image Source: https://www.quantstart.com/articles/Bayesian-Statistics-A-Beginners-Guide/

If this equation makes your eyes glaze over, don't worry. The entire point of this chapter is to attempt to make Bayes' Rule more understandable for those just getting started. Let's work through some concrete examples to give some context to this equation. Seeing some real-world applications to sports modelling probability should help to make sense of what might otherwise appear to be a confusing clump of letters and brackets.

BAYES' RULE APPLICATION EXAMPLES

Question 1: MLB team X has a 58% win rate over the course of the season. Their starting pitcher for tonight has a 63% win rate in games that he starts. How can we adjust our expected win percentage for team X in light of this new pitcher information?

From a conceptual perspective, we know that what we're trying to do here is update our prior beliefs in the face of new information. So our team X win probability of 58% in this case represents our "prior" (or pre-existing) belief about team X's win percentage. It's the belief we have before we are presented with new evidence. Discovering that team X's starting pitcher has a 63% win rate is our new information - the information that would encourage us to update our previous (or prior) belief about team X's winning percentage tonight. When we update our belief about team X's winning percentage by incorporating this new information, we now have a new belief - which in Bayesian terms is called the "posterior probability". So our new belief is the result of our prior belief, modified by the discovery of new evidence.

Let's get back to our concrete example. Hopefully you're with me so far. Our inputs in the fact pattern are:

(Prior Belief) Team X Win Percentage: 58%

(New Evidence) Team X Starting Pitcher Win Percentage: 63%

New Belief: ?

Of course, our prior belief and new evidence also both imply the probability of losing too, so let's write that down as well:

Implied Team X Losing Percentage: 42%

Implied Starting Pitcher Losing Percentage: 37%

That should be everything we need. We're now we're ready to plug numbers into the formula and calculate what our new belief should be.

Let's name our 4 variables as follows:

Team X Win = A (58%)

Team X Loss = B (42%)

Starting Pitcher Win = C (63%)

Starting Pitcher Loss = D (37%)

Our transposed Bayes' Rule equation then looks like this:

New Belief = (A*C)/((A*C)+(B*D))

New Belief = (0.58*0.63)/((0.58*0.63)+(0.42*0.37))

New Belief = 70.16%

So our posterior probability, given our new evidence, becomes 70.16% for team X. Now, this is not a game forecast because we've only considered one team, but it does give you a fairly approachable example of how Bayesian belief updating works.[4]

Suppose we performed the same calculation on team X's opponent (let's call them team Y) and calculate their expected win rate, based on the new evidence of their respective starting pitcher, to be 61%. Can we do something to make these team probabilities sum to 100% in a way that makes sense for a game forecast?

Absolutely. The most straightforward way to convert these two probabilities to a game prediction would be to use a Bradley Terry paired comparison formula like so[5]:

Team X Win % = (team X win % / (team X w% + team Y w%))

Team Y Win % = (team Y win % / (team Y w% + team X w%))

Team X = (0.7016/(0.7016+0.61) = 53.49%

Team Y= (0.61/(0.61+0.7016) = 46.51%

So in this case team X has an estimated 53.49% chance of victory after factoring in their opponent's probabilities. You could do something similar to this for starting goalies in the NHL as well.

Let's try a different example.

Question 2: Your model predicts team X to have a 56% win probability in an upcoming game, but your model is only correct 48% of the time. How should you adjust your confidence in team X's chances to win?

Once again, we have a prior belief and some new evidence that would suggest we should update our belief. Let's name our variables to keep things simple:

Predicted Team X Win = A (56%)

Predicted Team X Loss = B (44%)

Model Win = C (48%)

Model Loss = D (52%)

We plug our numbers into the formula as follows:

New Belief = (A*C)/((A*C)+(B*D))

New Belief = (0.56*0.48)/((0.56*0.48)+(0.44*0.52))

New Belief = 54.02%

We can see here that using Bayes' Rule, our confidence in the model's projected probabilities should be tempered a bit, which makes intuitive sense.

While this has been the lightest of crash courses, hopefully you've found this short explanation useful. I'd encourage you to experiment with the concepts presented, and consider reading more about Bayesian statistical methods generally. A great book to get you started is "Bayesian Statistics The Fun Way" by Will Kurt.

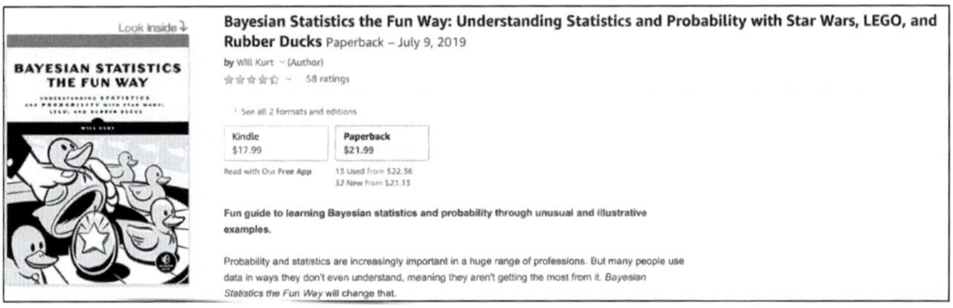

---

1. https://www.quantstart.com/articles/Bayesian-Statistics-A-Beginners-Guide/
2. I would recommend you read the article from endnote 1 in this chapter to learn more about how Bayes' Rule is transposed into a more useful form for our purposes. It's an excellent read.
3. https://towardsdatascience.com/can-you-accurately-predict-mlb-games-based-on-home-and-away-records-8a9a919bad29
4. It's also arguably not a game forecast because all we're using here are basic team win percentages, but that's besides the point.
5. We could also use something like Bill James' log5 method as well. It's very similar.

16

SEEKING RISK, TILTING & STAKES

This section of the book contains some thoughts on various sports betting topics which are anecdotal, speculative or of the N=1 variety. I have included these elements because I believe they will be useful for you, or at least thought provoking.

SEEKING RISK

In Scot's Gaelic there is a saying:

"Na sir, 's na seachan an cath"

"Neither seek out nor shun battle"

While you can rest assured that the intent of this Hebridean maxim was likely to speak about actual battle, it nonetheless contains a great deal of transferability to a sports bettor's ideal relationship with risk taking.

People as a general rule are either timidly risk adverse or impetuously risk seeking in nature. Effective risk management requires you to fight the urges of either extreme - you must strive to be comfortable with risk when the estimated rewards justifies it but not seek it out recklessly for its own sake. This takes practice.

You may remember a time when you really wanted to bet that day, before even knowing what calculated edges might exist. The desire for action preceded the rational basis. This is the "seeking out battle" misstep from our Gaelic proverb. You may also remember a time when you had a calculated edge, but for one reason or another decided against placing a proportional amount of your bankroll at risk. Risk aversion, for one reason or another, hindered your ability to make the correct decision. This would be the "shunning battle" misstep.

The ideal mindset, of course, is to try and be balanced, ready to capitalize on opportunity when it presents itself, but not trying to force a bet when there isn't a clear edge. In my opinion this can only come with experience and concerted efforts to apply your process in a disciplined way. When you find yourself leaning towards either extreme, it's time to pause and reflect.

Assess the market and look for value, cognizant that sometimes (frequently) there is little to be found. Some days the correct play is "no bets today". Other days it's $1,500 on a mispriced player prop. *Neither seek nor shun battle.*

GOING ON TILT

"Tilt" is a term that comes from poker (or pinball originally), and refers to making bad decisions as a result of heightened emotional states (either positive or negative). The ever helpful Wikipedia has this to say about tilting:

> The most common cause of tilt is losing, especially being defeated

> in a particularly public and humiliating fashion. In poker, a bad beat can upset the mental equilibrium essential for optimal poker judgment, causing frustration...
>
> ...though not as commonly acknowledged or discussed, it is also quite possible to go on "winner's tilt" as a result of a *positive* trigger: such as winning unexpectedly, or going on a string of good luck. Strong positive emotions can be just as dizzying and detrimental to one's play as negative ones. Tilting and winner's tilt can both lead to the same habits[1].

As a sports bettor, you already know what *going on tilt* is. It's that feeling of discomfort and agitation when you lose. It's also that rush of endorphins and feeling of invulnerability when you win or go on a hot streak.

Going on tilt, either from winning or losing, is a factor that can lead to failing the "neither seeking or shunning battle" test in a way that is harmful to both your mental acuity and your bankroll. Make no mistake, the worst bets you are ever likely to make are after a big loss or after a big win.

STAKING SIZE

Enter bankroll management *raison d'être* number 2 - to keep you in the mental state most optimal for making good decisions.

The correct staking size is one that keeps you in the game long enough to figure out if you have a reasonable expectation of profit AND one that doesn't invoke strong emotional responses that would affect your mental state in the event of either a win or a loss. Yes this will also shield you from the risk of ruin, and yes, it will also (hopefully) give you enough trials for your perceived edge to take hold. Most importantly though, if your bets are sized correctly, it will help to prevent you from going on tilt.

The key takeaway here is that part of a successful betting strategy is finding ways to reduce the variance of your reaction to your betting results. With experience you will become more comfortable with risk. In the meantime, the idea is to train yourself to feel the ups and downs less severely so that you remain focused on your process and emotionally unswayed by outcomes. This will keep you in the ideal position to make good decisions.

Focusing on process instead of results. Remaining emotionally balanced in the face of wins and losses. Neither needlessly seeking nor avoiding risk.

These things will help you on your way. Size your stakes to facilitate these elements.

---

1. https://en.wikipedia.org/wiki/Tilt_(poker)

17

WHAT'S NOT IN THE LINE?

Chances are good that if you're new to sports modelling, you're still watching games from a fan perspective. You're looking for the action. You're watching where the ball or puck moves. You're waiting to see team X score.

There's nothing wrong with that of course, but I've found that the more sports modelling work I do, the more I view the individual games differently.

I've stopped watching the ball.[1]

WATCHING THE GAME LIKE A DETECTIVE

You might consider what I'm about to say as akin to the philosophy of expected goals [xG]. Outside of the exciting parts of any game - the goals, the dunks, the 98 yard return touchdowns - there are underlying factors within a team's control that are more predictive of future outcomes than actual goals or points. We understand this as modellers. These are the parts of the game many fans overlook.

Some of them are less quantifiable than others.

These are the defensive tendencies. The player movement on a pick and roll. The effectiveness of a 2-1-2 forecheck. These are all elements of a game that are within a team's control that create scoring chances. Not all of them are perfectly incorporated into the current betting line.

Watching games and taking notes on player and team tendencies that aren't easily converted to numbers can provide a source of insight that guides your betting. An NBA center might be facing a hated rival and therefore have a higher probability of fouling out of the game. A starting pointguard may have a tendency to roll left on a pick and roll which presents an opportunity for a defender who is strong on that side to block more shots.

Viewing the game like a detective searching for predictive clues like this can assist your process greatly.

In the search for undiscovered sources of potential value, the question is:

> "What's not in the line?"

While it's true that the line for most major sports aggregates a tremendous amount of information, there remains a possibility that little bits of helpful insight haven't been perfectly incorporated.

If you watch the games as a detective rather than a fan, you may just find one.

---

1. This is primarily in regards to the ball/puck in basketball, soccer, football and hockey. Not so much in baseball. You're probably still going to want to watch the ball there.

18

WHERE TO FIND DATA

Finding decent (and free) sources of data for your sports modelling efforts can often be a challenge. With that in mind, here are some available sources of both paid and free data that you may wish to consider.

HISTORICAL ODDS DATA

Sportsbook Reviews Online [Free]

https://www.sportsbookreviewsonline.com/scoresoddsarchives/scoresoddsarchives.htm

Indatabet [Paid]

https://www.indatabet.com

SBR Odds [Free]

https://www.sportsbookreview.com/betting-odds/

NHL DATA

Hockey Reference [Free]

Hockey-reference.com

Natural Stat Trick [Free]

https://www.naturalstattrick.com

Big Data Ball [Paid]

https://www.bigdataball.com/datasets/

NBA DATA

Basketball Reference [Free]

Basketball-reference.com

Big Data Ball [Paid]

https://www.bigdataball.com/datasets/

NBA Official [Free]

https://stats.nba.com/leaders/

NFL DATA

Big Data Ball [Paid]

https://www.bigdataball.com/datasets/

Pro Football Reference [Free]

Pro-football-reference.com

Armchair Analysis [Paid]

https://www.armchairanalysis.com

ENGLISH PREMIER LEAGUE DATA

Football Data UK [Free]

http://www.football-data.co.uk

FB Reference [Free]

https://fbref.com/en/

NCAAB DATA

Sports Reference CBB [Free]

https://www.sports-reference.com/cbb/

Jeff Sagarin Ratings NCAAB [Free]

https://www.usatoday.com/sports/ncaab/sagarin/

19

WRAPPING UP

We've been over a number of different types of models in this book that, while not ground breaking, can definitely assist you in developing your own process. I hope that the provided examples have been useful to you in this respect.

Always try to remember, a model is just a tool. Ideally, it acts as a safeguard against our own most deleterious cognitive biases. It's there to make sure that we are starting from a reasonable place, to improve decision making, but not to entirely replace it.

Ultimately, we are still required to think.

Best of luck in your future sports modelling endeavours.

~ **Andrew Mack**

ABOUT THE AUTHOR

Andrew Mack is a JD/MSc Data Science student and sports bettor. As a former Journeyman Electrician, he has a passion for using applied math to solve problems.

He has been modelling sports since 2012 and has experience with statistical & machine learning models in Excel, R and Python for most major sports including the NBA, NFL, NHL, MLB, AFL and the English Premier League. Andrew holds an undergraduate degree in social sciences from the University of Victoria and lives in Calgary, Alberta, Canada.

He can be reached on twitter **@Gingfacekillah**.

ACKNOWLEDGMENTS

The author would like to thank the following people on Twitter for their contribution to publicly available sports modelling, statistical and sports betting knowledge:

@12Xpert

@MatterOfStats

@PlusEVAnalytics

@octonion

@willkurt

@MikePodhorzer

@Quantum_Sport

@EdMillerPoker

@optibrebs

@opisthokonta

@truepokerjoe

@jakevdp

@thepowerrank

@Toirtap

@Tangotiger

@drob

ALSO BY ANDREW MACK

BOOKS

Statistical Sports Models in Excel Volume 1

PODCASTS

Pinnacle Podcast - A Guide To Modelling in Sports Betting

https://soundcloud.com/pinnacle-podcast/a-guide-to-modelling-in-sports-betting

Pinnacle Podcast - Profit From Perspective

https://soundcloud.com/pinnacle-podcast/profit-from-perspective-with-andrew-mack

Business of Betting Podcast - Modelling, Statistics & Bayes' Theorem

https://businessofbetting.libsyn.com/ep-120-betting-with-modeling-statistics-and-bayes-theorem

Chilling With Charlie Podcast - Sports Modelling

https://podcasts.apple.com/us/podcast/ep-25-sports-modelling-with-gingfacekillah-andrew-mack/id1455613899?i=1000446224635

Champion Bets Podcast - Learning To Win

https://www.championbets.com.au/betting-360-podcast/ep-161-learning-win-sport-andrew-mack/

ARTICLES

Pinnacle - Failure: The Secret To Success?

https://www.pinnacle.com/en/betting-articles/Betting-Strategy/failure-success-in-betting/4QG2FQMBKNU7A8PA

Printed in Germany
by Amazon Distribution
GmbH, Leipzig

22491766R00086